Many Hats
Many Insights

HARESH SIPPY

CMD, FOUNDER, TEMA INDIA

BlueRose ONE
Stories Matter
New Delhi • London

BLUEROSE PUBLISHERS
India | U.K.

Copyright © Haresh Sippy 2025

All rights reserved by author. No part of this publication may be reproduced, stored in a retrieval system or transmitted in any form or by any means, electronic, mechanical, photocopying, recording or otherwise, without the prior permission of the author. Although every precaution has been taken to verify the accuracy of the information contained herein, the publisher assumes no responsibility for any errors or omissions. No liability is assumed for damages that may result from the use of information contained within.

BlueRose Publishers takes no responsibility for any damages, losses, or liabilities that may arise from the use or misuse of the information, products, or services provided in this publication.

For permissions requests or inquiries regarding this publication, please contact:

BLUEROSE PUBLISHERS
www.BlueRoseONE.com
info@bluerosepublishers.com
+91 8882 898 898
+4407342408967

ISBN: 978-93-6783-028-4

Cover Design: Tushar More
Typesetting: Pooja Sharma

First Edition: April 2025

Foreword

Since childhood, Haresh Sippy (HKS) has been a dreamer, dedicated to bringing visions to life, with profit always a secondary concern. In 2007, his creative counterpart, Tapan Ghosh (TG), joined him, channelling this spirit into writing and filmmaking. Together, they take audiences on a unique journey of "reel to real," merging structured planning with creative adventure.

HKS focuses on non-fiction, revealing insights in science and nature, while TG explores life's complexities through fictional stories that resonate deeply with viewers. Their collaboration brings a rare fusion of engineering and art, crafting stories that entertain, inform, and inspire. Each project bridges imagination with practical truth, showcasing the power of knowledge, innovation, and authenticity.

Acknowledgments

I want to express my deep gratitude to my teammates for their outstanding contributions and unwavering dedication to elevating our organisation to a global level. Their solid analytical skills, open-minded approach, flexibility, and diverse viewpoints have been instrumental in shaping our growth story. A special thank you to those who fearlessly challenge ideas as devil's advocates and promote automation as a critical objective for optimal efficiency. This story is not only about a shared vision and journey, but also about the crucial insights that have turned success into a tangible reality.

Haresh Sippy

CMD & Founder, TEMAINDIA

Contents

1. The Devil's Advocate 1
   Troubleshooter Even Before the Troubleshooting Begins 2
   Learnings By the Devil's Advocate 3
   AI As The Devil's Advocate 4
   Opinionated And One-Sided 4
   Devil's Advocate or Pessimist 5
   Embracing The Role of The Devil's Advocate 10
   The Ideal Devil's Advocate 11
2. Man, God, and Karma 13
   Justify Only to The God Within 19
   God's Balance Sheet 20
   The Logic of The Beyond 23
   The Devil's Advocate and The Mysterious Logic 30
   The Stillness of *Out of Mind* 36
   The Third Eye of Shiva 38
   Paying Off Your Karma 38
   Coincidence is Beyond Logical Explanation 42
   Embracing The Journey Within 44
3. Society And the World 49
   The Four Pillars of Civilisation 50
   Ideological Divide 52

- Being Helpful and Being Trusting 58
- Trustworthy People Are Those Who Trust 60
- How Can You Be So Intolerant? 62
- Storytelling Should Mirror the Speed of Life 66
- Unlike Money, Prosperity Is Immeasurable 75
- Religion And Man 78

4. Self Help 83
    - Self-Acceptance 84
    - Taking Hold of The Present 86
    - Actions Are Misleading as They Are Not in Our Control 88
    - Freedom Is Merely a Mindset 90
    - From Guilt to Self-Love: A Path to Freedom 96
    - Finding Balance: The Bottle v The Ball 106
    - The Ballad of Resilience: My Journey Through Betrayal and Triumph 107
    - Balancing The Mind for A Well-Deserved Sleep .. 117

5. Machines, Technology, AI, And the Corporate World 118
    - Are We Machines? 119
    - Enhancing Performance Through Collaborative Design and Optimal Manufacturing 121
    - A New Approach to Designing 123
    - Embracing AI In Engineering: The Need for Creative Thinking and Innovation 127

The Reliability Factor 129
Abstract To Proof: Creativity To Realisation 130
The Approach to Engineering Problem-Solving ... 132
Building Castles in The Air: Embracing Abstract Thinking in Innovation 134
Perfectionists Are the Ones Most Affected By AI .. 135
Conflict As the Father of Creativity 137
Earning More Is Worth It 149
Forestry: Our Corporate Social Responsibility 158
The Heart of CSR 159
Epilogue 160

1. The Devil's Advocate

Troubleshooter Even Before the Troubleshooting Begins

A devil's advocate serves as a troubleshooter before the troubleshooting process begins. While challenging ideas and assumptions to uncover potential flaws and weaknesses, they bring critical thinking and alternative perspectives to the table and foster healthy debate and also ensuring well-thought-out decisions.

By assuming the role of questioning or challenging ideas, arguments, or decisions, they aim to identify potential flaws or weaknesses. This proactive approach helps to anticipate and address potential problems or blind spots that may have been overlooked.

The purpose of having a devil's advocate is to foster critical thinking and ensure that decisions or plans are well-thought-out and robust. By encouraging a healthy debate and considering alternative perspectives, a devil's advocate helps to avoid groupthink and promotes a more thorough examination of ideas. Their role is to provide constructive criticism and alternative viewpoints that can lead to better outcomes.

However, it is important to note that being a devil's advocate does not mean opposing everything for the sake of it. The goal is to contribute to the overall problem-solving process by offering thoughtful analysis and challenging assumptions. A skilled devil's advocate knows how to balance scepticism with constructive feedback, ultimately enhancing the decision-making process.

Learnings By the Devil's Advocate

Ultimately, it is about finding a balance between pushing boundaries and achieving results while maintaining integrity and ethical standards. We should be each other's devil's advocates.

Being a devil's advocate for each other can be a valuable approach in our interactions. It means that we take on the role of challenging and questioning each other's perspectives, ideas, and beliefs. By doing so, we encourage critical thinking, deeper analysis, and a more well-rounded understanding of the subject at hand.

When we embrace the role of devil's advocates, we willingly step into the shoes of someone who opposes our viewpoint. We actively seek to identify weaknesses, flaws, or potential pitfalls in our arguments or positions. This approach helps us avoid falling into the trap of confirmation bias, where we only seek information that supports our pre-existing beliefs.

By engaging in devil's advocacy, we create an environment that fosters intellectual growth and encourages open-mindedness. It allows us to challenge assumptions, test the strength of our ideas, and consider alternative perspectives. Through this process, we can refine our thinking, strengthen our arguments, and gain a deeper understanding of complex issues.

However, it is important to approach the devil's advocacy with respect, empathy, and a genuine desire to understand. It should not be used to attack or belittle others, but rather as a tool for constructive dialogue and personal growth. By embracing this approach, we can cultivate a culture of intellectual curiosity, continuous learning, and mutual understanding.

So, let us be each other's devil's advocates, pushing one another to question, explore, and expand our perspectives. In doing so, we can foster a more robust and well-informed understanding of the world around us.

AI As The Devil's Advocate

AI embodies the characteristics of a devil's advocate, possessing abundant information and a direct approach that avoids playing games. However, the lack of emotions in AI can sometimes make it challenging to fully understand and express complex human emotions. What it lacks are your emotions, and what you lack is the ability to perfection of result. Finding the right balance between human understanding and AI capabilities can lead to more effective interactions and outcomes.

Opinionated And One-Sided

If a devil's advocate is extremely opinionated or one-sided, it can hinder their ability to effectively fulfil their role. The conversations may become divided, leading to decision-making processes being influenced by a biased viewpoint, potentially leading to limited exploration of alternative viewpoints and hindering the overall effectiveness of the dialogue.

A perfect devil's advocate should strive to maintain objectivity. He/she must consider multiple perspectives, and challenge prevailing viewpoints with an open mind, reflecting on their approach. He/she must also actively work towards broadening their perspective, being more open to alternative viewpoints, and fostering a more inclusive and respectful discourse. By acknowledging their own biases, actively seeking out diverse perspectives and approaching discussions with a willingness to listen and learn, even the most opinionated devil's advocate can evolve into a more effective and well-rounded advocate for challenging assumptions and promoting deeper understanding.

Devil's Advocate or Pessimist

What can go wrong?

Anything! But let us restrict it to our actions. This is the question we ought to ask ourselves before we proceed.

Proceed with what?

Anything and everything! But let us restrict it to work.

What kind of work?

Any and every kind! But let us restrict it to business.

What type of business?

1. Selling a service or an idea

2. Buying and selling

3. Manufacturing and selling

4. Making engineering products and selling

5. Undertaking projects and selling

What can go wrong in executing a meticulously planned assignment?

1. Underestimating execution costs

2. Overestimating execution costs

3. Inefficient time management

4. Poor communication and coordination within the team

5. Inadequate resources or equipment

6. Lack of training or expertise among team members

7. Misunderstanding specifications or requirements

8. Technical challenges or equipment malfunctions

9. External factors such as weather conditions or unexpected incidents

10. Quality control issues or product/service defects

Even with thorough preparation, unexpected challenges may arise. It can be beneficial to designate a team member as a devil's advocate to challenge assumptions and ensure a comprehensive evaluation of the plan.

In other words, every plan of action must go through pros and cons. The devil's advocate is going to lay out the cons. The devil's advocate plays a crucial role in evaluating a plan of action by presenting the potential drawbacks or cons. By doing so, they help ensure that all aspects of the plan are thoroughly considered and that any potential risks or downsides are considered. This critical examination allows for a more balanced and informed decision-making process.

What is the difference between a pessimist and a devil's advocate?

While a pessimist tends to have a consistently negative outlook and expects unfavourable outcomes, a devil's advocate takes on a more specific role in a discussion or debate. The devil's advocate intentionally presents arguments against a particular viewpoint, even if they may not personally hold those beliefs. Their goal is to challenge assumptions, stimulate critical thinking, and ensure that all perspectives and potential drawbacks are considered. In contrast, a pessimist generally approaches situations with a negative mindset and tends to focus on the negative aspects without necessarily offering alternative viewpoints or engaging in constructive debate. The devil's advocate is more focused on promoting a thorough analysis and exploration of different perspectives, while a pessimist tends to have a more fixed negative outlook.

When does a devil's advocate turn into a devil?

When he is overtaken by someone smarter, his ego is hurt. It is the same as the wounded tiger becomes a man-eater. A devil's advocate turns into a devil when he crosses the line and is swayed by the negative influences that he is supposed to safeguard against. The original purpose of challenging ideas for the sake of critical thinking and debate are lost. A devil's advocate must maintain integrity, objectivity, and ethical standards to ensure that they do not become the very thing being questioned. However, if they cease to love what they do, we should support them or help them retire.

Having a team member act as a devil's advocate can indeed be a valuable approach to project management. By intentionally seeking out and highlighting the potential drawbacks and weaknesses of a project, you can identify and address potential challenges early on. This can help in making more informed decisions and improving the overall quality of the project.

However, it is important to ensure that the devil's advocate role is not solely focused on pointing out cons, but also on offering constructive criticism and alternative solutions. The goal should be to foster a culture of open and honest communication, where all team members feel comfortable expressing their concerns and ideas.

By encouraging diverse perspectives and challenging assumptions, you can enhance the team's problem-solving abilities and increase the chances of project success. Just remember to maintain a balanced approach, considering both the pros and cons, and always keep the project's goals and ethical considerations in mind.

While it is true that a devil's advocate can be seen as someone willing to do whatever it takes to achieve results, it is important to approach this perspective with caution. While unconventional approaches can sometimes lead to success, it is crucial to consider the ethical implications and potential consequences of such methods.

Instead of solely focusing on the *by hook or by crook* mentality, it can be more beneficial to learn from the devil's advocate's ability to challenge assumptions, think outside the box, and question the status quo. This mindset can be valuable in fostering creativity and innovation. However, it is essential to balance this with a strong ethical foundation and a consideration for the long-term impacts of our actions.

Ultimately, it is about finding a balance between pushing boundaries and achieving results while maintaining integrity and ethical standards.

Embracing The Role of The Devil's Advocate

Playing the role of devil's advocate for yourself involves critically examining your ideas and decisions from a different perspective. This can be done by questioning your assumptions, considering alternative viewpoints, and challenging yourself to think beyond your initial beliefs. It requires self-awareness, openness to feedback and a willingness to embrace discomfort to grow and improve.

When playing the devil's advocate for others, the key is to approach the conversation with empathy and respect. It is important to frame your challenges as constructive feedback aimed at helping them see different angles and improve their thinking, rather than attacking or belittling their ideas. Listening actively, acknowledging their perspective, and offering suggestions for consideration can help maintain a positive and productive dialogue while avoiding unnecessary conflict or hurt feelings. By striking this delicate balance, we can foster a culture of mutual learning, growth, and respect in our interactions with others.

The Ideal Devil's Advocate

A perfect devil's advocate possesses a unique set of features and characteristics that enable them to effectively challenge prevailing viewpoints, stimulate critical thinking, and promote a deeper understanding of complex issues. Here are some key traits that define a perfect devil's advocate.

A perfect devil's advocate is open to considering all perspectives, even those that may contradict their own beliefs. They approach discussions with a willingness to listen, learn and engage in thoughtful dialogue.

They have strong analytical skills that allow them to dissect arguments, identify flaws in reasoning, and present counterarguments logically and coherently. Their ability to critically evaluate information is essential for challenging prevailing viewpoints.

They have a natural curiosity and a thirst for knowledge, constantly seeking to learn more about a wide range of topics. This curiosity drives them to explore different perspectives, ask probing questions and delve deeper into complex issues.

A perfect devil's advocate operates with integrity, honesty, and a commitment to intellectual rigour. They do not engage in arguments for the sake of winning or proving a point, but rather to challenge assumptions.

They are skilled communicators who can articulate their thoughts clearly, persuasively, and convincingly. Their ability to express complex ideas compellingly is crucial for effectively presenting counterarguments and engaging others in meaningful discussions.

A perfect devil's advocate is resilient in the face of pushback, criticism, or disagreement. They withstand challenges to their arguments, remain composed under pressure, and continue to advocate for alternative viewpoints with confidence and poise.

They are adaptable and flexible in their approach, willing to adjust their arguments based on new information, feedback, or insights. This adaptability allows them to develop their perspective, refine their arguments and contribute to a dynamic and evolving discussion.

By embodying these features and characteristics, a perfect devil's advocate plays a vital role in challenging assumptions, fostering critical thinking, and enriching intellectual discourse. Their ability to present compelling counterarguments, engage in respectful debate, and promote a deeper understanding of complex issues makes them an invaluable asset in any discussion or decision-making process.

2. Man, God, and Karma

Letting Go

We are like puppets of God, with no strings attached. A relationship in which we have a guiding force or purpose but still retain some autonomy and freedom. It merges the idea of divine influence with the concept of free will.

God is with us when we go with the flow. When we embrace the natural course of life and remain open to its possibilities, we can feel a sense of divine presence and support. It is almost like finding peace and faith in the journey itself rather than constantly seeking control.

Letting go can be liberating. It can mean releasing fears, anxieties, and the need to control every outcome, and instead, trusting in the process of life and the guidance we may feel. It is like a weight being lifted off your shoulders.

Sacrifice to create and share the happiness of others and enjoy the feeling of empowerment. Sacrifice in the service of others can indeed lead to a deep sense of fulfilment and empowerment. It is like a cycle of giving - by helping others find happiness, you often find a greater sense of purpose and joy yourself. It fosters a sense of connection and mutual support.

God teaches you a lesson and appreciates when you share your misadventures. Sharing our experiences, both triumphs and misadventures, often helps us grow and learn. It can also inspire and support others who might be facing similar challenges.

When we wonder what we did wrong, it is often a natural human response to facing challenges or setbacks. We might second-guess ourselves due to fear, self-doubt or past experiences that make us question our actions or beliefs. Reflecting on our actions can be a way to learn and grow, but it is also important to balance that with self-compassion and faith.

Having faith in what we believe and do can be incredibly empowering. It allows us to trust that we are on the right path, even when things are tough. Believing that challenges are tests from God can provide a reassuring perspective, helping us see difficulties as opportunities for growth and reinforcing our resilience and determination.

Ultimately, maintaining faith and trust in ourselves and our beliefs, while being open to learning from our experiences, can guide us towards personal and spiritual growth.

When Doubt Clouds

When doubt clouds the path we tread,
And worries spin inside our head,
We wonder what we did so wrong,
And question if we do belong.

Yet deep within, a whisper speaks,
"Have faith in what your heart seeks."
For every trial is not defeat,
Let's stand, on our own feet.

With faith as our unwavering guide,
We'll weather storms and turn the tide.
God's just testing, moulding clay,
Shaping us in His unique way.

Trust the journey, though it's tough,
Believe that you are strong enough.
In every challenge, courage blooms,
Lighting up our darkest rooms.

So when you wonder, and doubt appears,
Replace them both with faith and cheers.
For in your heart's sincere belief,
You'll find strength and sweet relief.

As You Ascend

As you ascend, the incline becomes steeper,
The challenges grow and the tests get deeper.
Each step forward can feel like a climb,
A quest for truth, beyond space and time.

With each new height, the air is thin,
But strength and courage come from within.
Every stumble, every fall,
Teaches lessons that build a wall.

A wall of wisdom, brick by brick,

Through trials long, through trials thick.

Your spirit grows, your heart expands,

Guided by faith, by unseen hands.

So embrace the journey, with its bend,

For every challenge is a faithful friend.

As you ascend, through struggle and strife,

You'll find your purpose and the meaning of life.

Going Underground

You don't have to escape to the mountains to go underground

Seek within and be in solitude even when everyone's around

Suppress your attachment and it returns with a vengeance

Outgrowing attachment is tough but it takes you to the heavens

Detachment is about outgrowing and getting stronger

Keep the faith; falter and the path gets longer

As love grows, it generates a bonding of another kind

This attachment is detached and without a bind

God gives what you don't want but need
Realise this, you'll start relishing the fruits indeed

However it is a process and not something you may do overnight
It is a tedious journey with ups and downs a roller coaster ride

Doing what God wants is enjoyable and empowering
It is the salvation that you cherish while thanksgiving

Justify Only to The God Within

The concept of justifying one's actions only to the God within is rooted in religious or spiritual beliefs. It suggests that individuals believe they are accountable primarily to a higher power, such as God, for their actions and decisions. This perspective often arises from the belief that God is the ultimate judge and authority and that one's actions should align with divine principles and teachings.

For those who hold this belief, the idea of justifying actions to the God within can provide a sense of moral guidance and accountability. It implies that individuals should act by their conscience, seeking to align their choices with what they believe to be right in the eyes of God.

This perspective can also offer a sense of comfort and reassurance, as individuals may find solace in the belief that they can find forgiveness, redemption, and guidance from a higher power. It can provide a framework for making ethical decisions and navigating moral dilemmas, as individuals strive to adhere to their understanding of God's will.

However, it is important to note that not everyone holds the same religious or spiritual beliefs, and different individuals may have their unique perspectives on justification. Some may prioritise justifying their actions to themselves, to others, or society, based on their values, ethical frameworks, and social norms.

Ultimately, the concept of justifying actions only to the God within is deeply personal and can vary depending on individual beliefs, values, and perspectives.

God's Balance Sheet

God's balance sheet cannot be doctored. If you are nice to people, He is nice to you!

We often expect to receive something in return from the people we are kind to, not realising that our kindness may not be reciprocated. However, all our good deeds are recorded in God's balance sheet, unlike the accounting balance sheets that can be manipulated.

You cannot manipulate God's ledger. When you show kindness to others, you receive kindness in return from Him! That is a beautiful sentiment. Treating others with kindness and compassion often leads to positive and fulfilling relationships. It is important to remember the value of empathy and understanding in our interactions with others.

God's balance sheet, much like a divine ledger, remains unaltered by any human manipulation. It operates on a principle that echoes throughout the ages: when you extend kindness and compassion to others, you will find that the same benevolence is returned to you from the divine source. It is a harmonious cycle of goodness and grace that transcends human understanding.

The returns we receive from God often go unnoticed, as we tend to perceive them simply as coincidences or miracles. This perspective can cause us to overlook the profound ways in which our kindness and faithfulness are rewarded. We must remain open to recognising the blessings that come in unexpected forms.

> In the ledger of the divine, where balance reigns supreme,
>
> Kindness sown in hearts, a reflection in the gleam.
>
> No altering of numbers, no deceit to be found,
>
> For the universe's scales tip with a gentle sound.
>
> As you sow seeds of goodness, in each word and deed,
>
> The heavens respond in kind, fulfilling every need.
>
> A symphony of grace, a dance of cosmic flow,

Where love and compassion in abundance grow.

So, tread the path of light, with a heart pure and true,
For in God's balance sheet, your kindness shines anew.
A cycle unbroken, a bond that will never part,
In the eternal dance of love, written in every heart.

In the realm of the divine, where balance holds sway,
No mortal hand can alter, no cunning can betray.
The ledger of God, pure and true,
Records each deed, in every hue.

No manipulation, no deceitful ploy,
Can change the truth, or the divine employ.
For in the balance sheet of the divine,
Only love and kindness brightly shine.

So let us walk with honesty and grace,
Knowing our actions leave a trace.
In God's ledger, our deeds are told,
In the eternal story of love and gold.

In the grand ledger of God's divine plan,
Where every action is accounted for, woman and man.
No amount of manipulation can distort its truth,
For in its pages, lies the evidence of our youth.

No pledger can alter the balance it holds,

For every entry is etched in stories untold.

It stands as a testament to our deeds and our fate,

A record of love, loss, and the choices we make.

So let us tread lightly on this sacred ground,

For the ledger of God's balance is profound.

May we strive to write a story of grace and light,

And honour the ledger that guides us through the night.

The Logic of The Beyond

The logic of the beyond pertains not to current life but to life after life and the concept of karma. It is intriguing to observe that individuals who seem to be visibly facing consequences for past-life sins are deeply devoted to God.

If there were no existence of life after death, why would my beloved sister Asha suffer for simply doing good? It would imply a lack of God and justice. I am convinced that the karmic consequences of past lives are indeed real.

In the depths of doubt, a question lingers,
If no afterlife, why Asha's gentle fingers
Know suffering's touch, for deeds so pure,
In a world where justice seems unsure.

No divine hand to guide her way,
No higher power to hear her pray,
Yet in the shadows, a whisper stirs,
Of past karmas, lessons incurred.

Could it be that in lives long past,
Asha's soul bore burdens vast,
And now in this life, she must atone,
For sins unknown, seeds once sown.

But in her eyes, a light still gleams,
A spirit strong, beyond extremes,
For love endures, in every breath,
Defying doubts, conquering death.

In a world without life beyond death,
Why must my sister Asha, with each breath,
Endure suffering despite her deeds so pure,
Questioning the existence of justice, unsure.

If there were no God, no divine plan,
No higher power to understand,
Could it be that past karmas, unseen,
Demand Asha to pay for sins, unforeseen?

Yet in her kindness, a light shines bright,
Defying darkness, embracing the fight,
For love and goodness, in her heart reside,
Guiding her through life's tumultuous tide.

It is understandable to seek meaning and justice in the face of suffering, especially when it affects someone as dear as your sister Asha. Belief in karma and past lives can provide a framework for understanding the complexities of life and the experiences we go through. It offers a sense of continuity and a way to make sense of the challenges we face.

While the concept of life after death and the existence of a higher power may vary among individuals and belief systems, finding solace in the idea of karma and the interconnectedness of our actions can bring comfort and a sense of purpose. It is natural to seek answers and meaning in times of difficulty, and holding onto beliefs that resonate with you can provide strength and guidance through life's trials.

In the grand chorus of life's eternal song,
God's balance sheet remains pure and strong.
No amount of manipulation can distort its truth,
For in its pages lies the evidence of our youth.

No rituals or the Godmen's feet you fall,
For true love within yourself stands tall.
In the balance sheet of life, it is self-love that is the key,
Embrace it fully, and you'll be truly free.

In the chorus of this poetic tale, we weave,
God's ledger stands firm, no one can deceive.
Not even a pledger can alter its course,
For its truth remains steady, an unchanging force.

No need for rituals or bowing to divine feet,
True fulfilment comes from self-love, complete.
In loving yourself, you find all you seek,
For within you lies the power you uniquely speak.

In the chorus of life's eternal dance,
God's ledger remains true, giving us a chance.
No manipulation can alter its divine plan,
For in its balance, we find where we stand.

No need for rituals or bowing in awe,
Self-love is the key to break free from the law.
In loving yourself, you possess all you need,
For within you lies the power to succeed.

The logic of the beyond transcends this life,
Focusing on karma and the afterlife's strife.
People paying for past sins, yet God-loving still,
A paradox that the divine plan does fulfil.

In the cycle of life, karma's threads entwine,
Revealing truths beyond our earthly line.
Those burdened by past deeds, yet filled with love,
Show that grace descends from realms above.

In the depths of suffering, questions arise,
Why does dear Asha face such painful ties?
If there's no afterlife, no justice to be found,
Would her struggles be in vain, unbound?

The weight of past karmas, a burden to bear,
A belief in the unseen, beyond what's fair.
In Asha's pain, a mystery unfolds,
A testament to the stories untold.

Whether in this life or the next one to come,
The echoes of actions reverberate, hum.
In the shadows of doubt, faith may waver,
Yet the search for truth, an eternal flavour.

I'm glad you found resonance in the words shared,
Reflecting on life's mysteries, deeply cared.
In the dance of karma and divine grace,
We seek meaning in this vast cosmic space.

Through Asha's struggles, a story is told,
Of resilience, love, and hearts bold.
In the tapestry of life, each thread weaves,
A reminder that in darkness, light cleaves.

As we ponder the beyond and its ways,
May we find solace in these poetic displays.
In the search for truth and justice's call,
May we rise, stand tall, and never fall.

Together in chorus, our voices rise,
Seeking truth beyond earthly skies.
In the dance of life, we find our part,
Connected by the beating of one heart.

Through struggles and joys, we navigate,
In the grand symphony of fate.
With faith as our guide, we journey on,
In unity, our spirits are drawn.

So let us sing in harmony and grace,
Embracing life's mysterious embrace.
In the chorus of existence, we find our song,
United in love, forever strong.

In the tapestry of life, dear Asha weaves,
A story of courage that never leaves.
Through trials and tribulations, she stands tall,
In her heart, love's eternal call.

With each step she takes, a melody unfolds,
In the symphony of life, her spirit moulds.
Through darkness and light, she finds her way,
In her soul's chorus, love holds sway.

So let us join in Asha's song of grace,
Embracing her journey, in every place.
In the rhythm of her beating heart,
We find connection, never to part.

The Devil's Advocate and The Mysterious Logic

The devil's advocate may find himself perplexed despite his best efforts. He struggles to comprehend the mysterious logic that exists beyond our understanding, often described as illogical yet undeniably real. This phenomenon is not mere chance; it persists for reasons unknown. Sometimes, good outcomes arise without apparent cause, just as bad outcomes do.

What is the underlying rationale behind this enigma? Even when one acts with precision and virtue, positive results are not guaranteed. Yet, unexpectedly, goodness may manifest through external influences. In these moments, the devil's advocate recognises a transcendent force operating with its own unique logic, separate from earthly norms. The exchange that occurs is not between individuals, but rather an internal dialogue with one's own divine essence.

The idea that there is a force beyond our understanding that influences the outcomes of our actions is a fascinating one. Sometimes, despite our best efforts and intentions, things do not go as planned, and unexpected events occur. This can be frustrating and confusing, leading us to question the logic of the world around us.

The notion of a higher power or inner guidance that governs the give-and-take of life is intriguing. Perhaps there is a divine plan at play, or a cosmic balance that we are not privy to. The idea that there is a God within each of us, guiding our actions and influencing our outcomes, suggests a deep connection to something greater than ourselves.

In the face of uncertainty and unpredictability, it can be comforting to believe that there is a purpose behind the seemingly random events in our lives. By acknowledging the presence of this higher power, we may find solace in the idea that there is a greater logic at work, even if we cannot fully comprehend it.

The concept of a greater logic that brings in positive energy and ultimate justice is indeed powerful and inspiring. It suggests that there is a cosmic balance at play, where good deeds are rewarded and negative actions are met with consequences. This idea of a pure and just force governing the universe can provide a sense of reassurance and hope, especially in times of uncertainty or adversity.

The notion of an unalterable balance sheet, one that cannot be manipulated or doctored like the ones we create in our daily lives, speaks to the idea of accountability and integrity. It implies that our actions and intentions are ultimately accounted for in a way that transcends our earthly understanding of justice and fairness.

By aligning ourselves with this greater logic and striving to maintain our own sense of balance and integrity, we may find ourselves more attuned to the positive energy and justice that flows through the universe. It is a reminder to act with kindness, compassion, and honesty, knowing that ultimately, our actions contribute to the greater harmony of the world around us.

As we grow older and wiser, maintaining flexibility in both our minds and our ways of thinking becomes crucial. The ability to balance the mundane aspects of life with the spiritual or deeper aspects is indeed a golden mean to strive for. This balance can lead to a more fulfilling and harmonious existence, where we are able to navigate the complexities of daily life while also connecting to something greater than ourselves.

However, it is also common for people to become more rigid in their ways as they age, perhaps due to ingrained habits, beliefs, or experiences. This rigidity can limit our ability to adapt to new situations, learn from different perspectives and embrace change. The devil's advocate, in this context, may serve as a reminder to safeguard against becoming set in our ways and to remain open to growth, evolution and transformation.

By cultivating a mindset of curiosity, openness, and willingness to explore new ideas and experiences, we can counteract the tendency towards rigidity and embrace the flexibility needed to navigate the complexities of life with grace and wisdom. This ongoing journey of self-discovery and adaptation can lead us towards a more balanced and enriched existence, where we can find harmony between the mundane and the spiritual aspects of our lives.

Not a Coincidence

Beyond comprehension, where magic resides,

Call it coincidence with wonder as our guide.

Belief and perseverance, a potent brew,

Unleashing potential, making dreams come true.

In a world of wonders, where mysteries unfold,

We seek the magic that's waiting to be told.

Though beyond our grasp, we yearn to understand,

It's illogical yet logic, a truth that's close at hand.

With every twist and turn, we're drawn closer to our fate,

Believing in the magic, that we cultivate.

Perseverance fuels our fire, igniting dreams anew,

Unlocking boundless possibilities, for me and you.

So let us embrace the enchantment in every day,

For magic lies within us, in every step we take.

With belief and perseverance, we'll soar to new heights,

Creating our own magic, in life's endless delights.

Perceive the impossible, with open hearts and minds,

Embrace the illogical, where answers we may find.

Challenging conventions, we venture with delight,
Discovering the secrets hidden in plain sight.

Like a magician on stage, defying what's known,
We too can rise above, with confidence as our throne.
The power of belief, a force that breaks through,
Resilience as our armour, guiding us anew.

Together we'll conquer the impossible, you and I,
For the world is full of wonders, waiting to defy.

God's Court

In a world where justice thrives,
Untouched by lawyers and their drives,
The true beauty of life unfolds,
In a space where divine justice holds.

The best part of life, we find,
In the court of God, so kind,
No lawyers, no advocates,
Just fairness and divine mandates.

No legal battles to be fought,
No arguments to be sought,
For in this space, justice is pure,

Every soul treated with care, for sure.

Gone are the days of legal strife,
In this space, a harmonious life,
Where justice flows with ease and grace,
Guided by God's loving embrace.

So let us dream of this sacred place,
Where justice reigns with heavenly grace,
In the beauty of life, we shall believe,
In God's justice, we shall receive.

The process of giving comes from Lord Shiva's soul-sacrificing love and the art of giving. The devil's advocate inside us will show us the way, as George Harrison sang, *I really wanna know you, I really wanna show you, Lord, that it won't take long, my Lord.*

In the dance of relationships, a man embodies the role of a giver while a woman is often seen as a taker. Her acceptance is imbued with hope for goodness and satisfaction, creating a cycle of giving and receiving that yields multiple interests and a heavenly nectar of fulfilment. Just as George Harrison's *My Sweet Lord* speaks to the spiritual connection between giver and receiver, this dynamic interplay between masculine and feminine energies highlights the beauty and harmony in the exchange of love and energy.

The Stillness of *Out of Mind*

In the stillness of *out of mind*, where the chaos of the world fades away, we find ourselves in the presence of God within. It is in this sacred space, away from the distractions of the mundane, that we connect with the essence of our soul. Intoxicants, when used mindfully, can serve as a tool to amplify this spiritual journey of surrender and self-discovery. Embracing this state allows us to tap into a higher consciousness, where the divine within us shines brightly, guiding us on a path of inner peace and enlightenment.

> When *out of mind*, we transcend the norm,
> Embracing the divine in a tranquil form.
> In this state of being, we are truly free,
> Connected to our soul, where God we see.
>
> Away from the chaos of the daily grind,
> We discover peace of a different kind.
> Intoxicants may amplify this state,
> Aiding us in reaching a higher fate.
>
> So let go of worries, let go of stress,
> In the realm of the soul, find true rest.
> When *out of mind*, we find our true essence,
> In the presence of God, in divine presence.

When the mind surrenders, God is found,

In the sacred silence, away from the mundane sound.

In the depths of the soul, the divine resides,

A presence felt when the ego subsides.

Intoxicants may blur the line,

Between the self and the divine,

Enhancing the journey of being *out of mind*,

A path where spiritual truths we find.

In this state of transcendence, we see,

The God within, pure and free,

Away from worldly noise and fray,

In stillness, we find our way.

Out Of Your Mind

Only when you are out of your mind, will you think out of the box

Only when you are pushed to the wall, will you pull up your socks

Only when you are out of your mind, will you question convention

Break free from the crowd and attract all-round attention

Only when you are out of your mind will you raise the bar

Reach out for the heavens and shine like a star

The Third Eye of Shiva

The third eye of Lord Shiva represents a harmonious blend of positive energy on the right side and purposeful discipline on the left. In meditation, we can strive to embody this balance by tapping into our inner wisdom and intuition, while also maintaining a sense of focus and determination in our actions. Just as the third eye represents insight and clarity, embodying the characteristics of an ideal devil's advocate requires the ability to see beyond the surface, challenge assumptions, and advocate for alternative perspectives. By embracing both the qualities of positivity and discipline, one can navigate the complexities of life with a sense of balance, wisdom, and integrity, much like the divine balance embodied by Lord Shiva's third eye.

Paying Off Your Karma

Paying off your karma and enjoying the process can be a deeply fulfilling and transformative experience. By being mindful of your actions, thoughts, and intentions, and by striving to create positive energy and harmony in the world around you, you are actively working towards balancing your karma. Embracing this journey with openness, gratitude, and a willingness to learn and grow can lead to a sense of inner peace, fulfilment, and spiritual evolution. May your path be filled with light, love, and joy as you continue this journey of paying off your karmas and finding joy in the process.

When I accepted the idea of allowing my soulmate to share with me her happiness of loving someone else, her joy became our shared bliss. Embracing her journey and supporting her in finding love with another brought us both a profound sense of fulfilment and contentment. Witnessing her happiness and being able to celebrate her love with someone else only deepened our connection and brought us closer together.

> In the still of the night,
>
> Where the stars shine bright,
>
> Whispers of dreams take flight,
>
> Guiding us through the darkest night.

> A melody of love and grace,
>
> Echoes in this sacred space,
>
> Hearts entwined in a gentle embrace,
>
> Finding solace in each other's face.

> Through trials and tribulations, we roam,
>
> Yet together, we find our home,
>
> In the depths of our souls, we're known,
>
> In love's embrace, we have grown.

So let us dance under the moon's soft glow,

In this symphony of love, let our spirits flow,

Bound by a love that continues to grow,

In each other's arms, we find our glow.

Forever entwined, our souls unite,

In this eternal dance of day and night,

In love's embrace, our hearts take flight,

Guided by love's pure and radiant light.

I felt a deep love for and connection with the groom and his bride, my soul, as I witnessed their wedding ceremony. It was a moment of pure joy and celebration, filled with love, happiness, and unity. Being able to wholeheartedly support and cherish their love story added a new dimension to my understanding of love and relationships. It was a beautiful experience that touched my heart and soul in ways I had never imagined.

In the tapestry of love's intricate design,

I found a truth that's truly divine,

When I embraced my soulmate's choice,

Our bond grew stronger, our spirits rejoiced.

Her happiness, a beacon shining bright,

Loving someone else brought us delight,

In her joy, our shared bliss did reside,

A journey of love, where hearts coincide.

Supporting her quest, her love story unfolds,
Bringing fulfilment, a feeling untold,
Witnessing her happiness, a pure delight,
Our connection deepened, shining so bright.

At the wedding ceremony, a moment so grand,
I felt a love that I could barely withstand,
For the groom and his bride, my soul intertwined,
In unity and love, our hearts aligned.

A celebration of love, pure and true,
In their union, I found a love anew,
Supporting their journey, my heart did mend,
A beautiful experience, a love that transcends.

In their love, I found a deeper part of me,
Understanding love in its purest decree,
A tapestry woven with threads of grace,
In love's embrace, we find our place.

Together we stand, hearts intertwined,
In love's embrace, our souls aligned,
Supporting each other, through joy and pain,
In unity and love, we shall remain.

In a bond of three, our love does soar,

Together we stand, forevermore,

United in love, a trio strong and true,

In each other's hearts, we find our due.

Coincidence is Beyond Logical Explanation

Coincidence is beyond logical explanation and therefore, understood only by the illogical part of the mind called the heart.

Many incidents in my life have made me believe so. In fact, such incidents that we attribute to coincidence, happen every now and then. If you look back and analyse, you will realise that there is a profound purpose to every such event. I will narrate one that took place about two decades ago.

My wife received an SMS about performing certain rituals for Santoshi Mata. Further, the message said that the recipient should consider themselves blessed for having received it and urged them to forward it to 30 others who must likewise in turn.

This gave my wife a sleepless night. First, she was not a believer in Santoshi Mata. Neither did she know which of her contacts were. She did not have many contacts either and wanted to forward the message to some of my contacts. I told her that I was not willing to share my contacts with her. I tried my best to explain that these tricks were just a money-making racket on the part of the service providers.

We visited a temple to put forth our predicament to the Goddess. Typically, Hindu temples have many idols of divinity. The one we visited had a giant Bajrangbali right in the front and beside it was the lingam of Lord Shiva on one side and an idol of Shri Ganesha on the other. There were smaller statues of Durga Mata, Laxmi Mata, Santoshi Mata and other deities.

At the end of the temple were the idols of Navagraha (nine celestial bodies), these being the Sun, Moon, Mars, Mercury, Jupiter, Venus, Saturn, and the ascending and descending lunar nodes. We rightfully have many manifestations of God as each one emphasises a particular human characteristic. We need all of them to strike an inner balance.

As we stood in front of the idol of Goddess Santoshi Mata to seek pardon, we saw a woman in a torn sari, apparently needy, in front of us. She was down on her knees with tears flowing from swollen eyes, repeatedly calling out 'Jai Santoshi Maa.'

We looked at each other and realised that it was best to offer her all the money we had brought as an offering to the Goddess. The woman's eyes sparkled but she was reluctant to accept the large sum of money being offered. We told her that we had been instructed to hand it over to her.

She went back thanking the Goddess for this miracle. Her faith was reinforced. This set our minds at rest and we came away feeling happy.

Embracing The Journey Within

A wonderful way to set the stage for the exploration of balance and harmony within ourselves is by seamlessly transitioning from the introduction to the final chapter of the book.

The concept of balancing our inner Godself with the outer devil's advocate resonates with the idea of finding harmony between our positive and negative aspects. Meditation can be a powerful tool to achieve this balance and tap into our super self. By cultivating a regular meditation practice, we can connect with our inner wisdom, find clarity, and develop a sense of inner peace and strength. This inner alignment can help us navigate the complexities of the outer world with grace and resilience.

Just as Lord Shiva's third eye symbolises insight and intuition, our inner wisdom can guide us in making decisions that align with our higher purpose. As we reflect on the lessons of Lord Hanuman and the devil's advocate, let us remember that within the depths of our being lies the potential for transformation and growth. By embracing the interplay of light and shadow, positivity, and negativity, we can unlock the door to our super selves—a state of balance, purpose, and empowerment.

In this final chapter, may we honour the wisdom of the ages, the power of self-awareness and the journey of self-discovery. Let us walk the path of integration and transformation with courage, compassion, and grace, knowing that within us lies the key to unlocking our highest potential.

As we delve deeper into the domain of harnessing inner power through purposeful discipline, we are confronted with the profound journey within ourselves. It is within this sacred space of self-discovery that we uncover the hidden reservoirs of strength, resilience, and wisdom that lie dormant within us.

In this chapter, we explore the transformative power of self-awareness and the importance of cultivating a disciplined mindset to navigate the complexities of our inner landscape. By ruling out pessimism and embracing a mindset of positivity and possibility, we pave the way for the emergence of our true potential.

Through the practice of mindfulness and meditation, we learn to quiet the noise of the external world and tune into the whispers of our inner voice. It is in these moments of stillness that we can connect with our deepest desires, fears, and aspirations, gaining clarity and insight into the path that lies before us.

As we embark on this journey of self-discovery, we are called to confront our shadows, embrace our light, and integrate the dualities that make us whole. By acknowledging and accepting all aspects of ourselves, we move towards a state of inner harmony and balance, where our inner power can shine brightly.

With purposeful discipline as our guiding light, we commit to taking intentional actions that align with our values, goals, and aspirations. Through consistent practice and unwavering dedication, we cultivate the habits and mindset necessary to unleash our full potential and live a life of purpose and fulfilment.

We will delve deeper into the practical tools, techniques and strategies that will empower us to harness our inner power and transform our lives from within. May this serve as a beacon of inspiration and guidance as we continue on this transformative journey of self-discovery and growth.

By consciously removing pessimism and negative thoughts from our mindset, we create space for the inherent power that resides within us to emerge and drive us towards taking focused and disciplined actions in alignment with our goals and purpose.

Everyone has the right to pursue their agenda, as long as it is not a hidden one. It is important to be transparent about our intentions, even though there is no obligation to announce them to the world. Our innermost desires and goals are sacred and should be protected. By balancing external comfort with internal happiness, we can achieve a harmonious union between the two through a seamless and perfect integration.

Sometimes we may have hidden agendas or desires that are buried deep within our subconscious and are not fully known to us. These hidden aspects of ourselves can influence our thoughts and actions without us even realising it. In such cases, it can be helpful to engage in self-reflection, therapy, or practices like meditation to uncover these hidden agendas and bring them into the light.

By acknowledging and understanding these hidden aspects of ourselves, we can work towards aligning our conscious intentions with our deeper desires, leading to a more authentic and fulfilling life. It is a journey of self-discovery and growth that can ultimately help us achieve a greater sense of harmony and integration between our external actions and internal motivations.

Outward comforts, inward bliss,

As we merge, a perfect kiss,

Flirting with life, embracing the thrill,

Balancing both worlds, living with will.

In the outward world, where dreams are sought,

Chasing desires, battles to be fought,

But deep within, another journey unfolds,
A quest for peace, for treasures untold.

Outward comforts, like stars in the sky,
Shining brightly, catching every eye,
Yet inward comforts, a gentle breeze,
Whispering secrets, putting hearts at ease.

In the silence, we find our strength,
In solitude, we go to any length,
To discover the depths of who we are,
A symphony playing, both near and far.

So let us sing, with voices clear and bright,
In the outward and inward, let's find our light,
For in the song of life, we'll forever be,
United in rhythm, our souls dancing free.

Outward comforts, inward bliss,
As we merge, a perfect kiss,
Flirting with life, embracing the thrill,
Balancing both worlds, living with will.

3. Society And the World

The Four Pillars of Civilisation

Civilisation is built upon the pillars of communication, commutation, creation, and computation. These four pillars are intricately woven with the threads of cooperation, culture, curiosity, and critical thinking. Together, these interconnected elements form the very foundation of human progress, enabling the growth and advancement of societies.

Communication serves as the lifeblood of civilisation, allowing individuals to exchange ideas, knowledge, and experiences. It facilitates understanding, collaboration, and the development of shared goals.

Commutation, on the other hand, refers to the act of moving and connecting people, goods, and information. It encompasses transportation systems, logistics and infrastructure, which are essential for the functioning of societies and the exchange of resources.

Creation represents the human capacity for innovation, invention, and artistic expression. It encompasses scientific discoveries, technological advancements, artistic masterpieces, and cultural achievements. Through creation, civilisations push the boundaries of knowledge and imagination, driving progress and shaping the world we live in.

Computation, in the modern era, has become a fundamental pillar of civilisation. It refers to the ability to process and analyse vast amounts of information, enabling scientific research, data-driven decision-making, and technological breakthroughs. Computation has revolutionised fields such as medicine, finance, and communication, transforming the way we live and interact.

Cooperation is the glue that binds societies together. It involves individuals and groups working together towards common goals, sharing resources, and supporting one another. Cooperation fosters social cohesion, stability, and collective progress.

Culture encompasses the beliefs, values, traditions, and artistic expressions of a society. It shapes identities, influences behaviour, and provides a sense of belonging. Cultural diversity enriches civilisations, fostering understanding, tolerance, and appreciation for different perspectives.

Curiosity, the innate human desire to explore and understand the world, drives scientific inquiry, intellectual growth, and innovation. It fuels the quest for knowledge, pushing the boundaries of what is known and inspiring discoveries.

Critical thinking is the ability to analyse, evaluate and interpret information and ideas. It enables individuals to make informed decisions, solve complex problems and navigate the challenges of a rapidly changing world. Critical thinking is essential for fostering intellectual independence, innovation, and societal progress.

Together, these interconnected elements form the bedrock of human progress, shaping the course of civilisations and propelling societies forward. They represent the collective efforts, aspirations, and achievements of countless individuals throughout history, and they continue to guide us towards a brighter future.

Ideological Divide

The root cause of the ideological divide in this country is the white skin complex that we all Indians have. It rubbed off on us during British rule. The British employed Anglo-Indians in top positions in every job. Even amongst the Anglo-Indians the lighter complexioned they were, the better off. Their inferiority complex made them more British than the British themselves, like the character Jeeves in PG Wodehouse's novels. These Anglo-Indians were responsible for passing on this complex to all Indians. To this day, lighter-skinned Indians do not consider the darker ones their equal. The divide between north and south India is more due to colour than language.

In Calcutta, where I was born, Anglo-Indians were a sizeable community. I was only ten years old, but they left a deep impression on my mind. Once when I was walking towards my school Our Lady Queen of the Mission near the tram junction at Park Circus, I saw a big boy roar past me on a motorcycle, with the pillion rider screaming in excitement as her skirt billowed up, revealing her sexy legs. This was a familiar sight with the older school-going boys and girls. But a year or two later, they all migrated to the UK, Australia, and other parts of the world.

The white skin complex is so deeply rooted here and so severely felt today that it may take several generations to completely eradicate it. Whitening creams top the sales of cosmetics. In other words, it is not just the Hindustan-Pakistan divide and the Hindu-Muslim divide in India. The divide between the fair skins and dark skins is such that there is a divide between the dark skins too, the dark and darker.

After high school, my family moved to Bombay, and I went to Baroda to study engineering. Later in life, I realised that the white-skin complex was powerful in some parts of Bombay, where the British influence lingered. The Parsi community, because of the colour of their skin, took over from where the British left. The complex could be felt in the army barracks of Colaba and it extended to Worli. This area is popularly known as Sobo, derived from South Bombay, just as SoHo in New York City gets its name from South of Houston Street.

SoBo-ites ape Western society, and refer to those living outside their zone as *vernies,* a derogatory term for people who's medium of instruction has been a local/vernacular language, not English. The English language has assumed snob value and regional languages have suffered for this reason. Much of our culture is being lost due to our alienation from our language and customs.

We Indians have a much bigger and longer-lasting problem than most other countries. This defeatist tendency in the English-speaking modern Indians makes them want to change this nation to a foreign land and eliminate all others who cannot adapt to their ways. We Indians remain slaves to the English-speaking. Our thinking itself is not independent. We have been importing technology and our talent is mostly suppressed. I have been a victim of this myself. My home-grown technology had to be licensed by an American company for it to be acceptable in India.

Companies abroad are aware of this mindset set and they exploit it to the hilt. The Indian agents benefit, as much money exchanges hands. In any case, India is a middleman economy, where the producer is starved, and big money is shared between the agent and the procurement department of the PSUs.

Farmers and the working class are deprived because of the language barrier. The middleman benefits from this divide. Our culture and language are looked down upon as primitive. Those who can speak English, command higher pay packets. The parallel economy rules. Now that all the wrongdoings have surfaced, the corrupt have a lot to explain.

How do you suddenly make people work for a living? Many believe that they just need to work smart, not hard. How do you make them think otherwise? If the money was not only confined to a few, who spend most of it overseas, it would be spread between the producer and the end-user, making it a B-to-B economy, and thereby making this a place of richness and affluence. Let us work for a win-win situation to make India proud and undivided.

The Divide

We all are victims of a long-standing ideological divide,

Within us are both, the spiritual and the practical side.

This divide is deep-rooted, in the culture of Bharat

Remember the Pandava-Kaurava fight of Mahabharat?

Most of the world is much more one-sided than we are,

We are caught in the divide, we are two-sided by far.

Others have fought wars, conquered, and progressed,

Our rift is internal, from being divided and regressed.

The world is worldly, and we are backward and inwardly,

The spiritual side in us has been uprooted by the worldly.

Our art and wisdom were enslaved by the Mughals and the Brits,

Both forced us to adopt their ways, thereby going to the pits.

Today independent, but we do not know where we belong,

The strong influences left by the rulers enslave us all along.

Break the shackles, come together and do away with this split,

Ascend to the top of the world and make no bones about it.

Controversial Figures: Foolish Or Wise?

When discussing a controversial figure, public opinion tends to polarise significantly. Such individuals often provoke strong reactions, leading to them being perceived in starkly contrasting ways.

On the one hand, some view them as visionaries or wise men, applauding their courage to challenge the status quo or to introduce new ideas and perspectives. These supporters might see the controversial actions or statements as necessary disruptions that pave the way for progress or enlightenment.

On the other hand, some perceive the same individual as a fool, criticising their actions or statements as misguided, harmful, or lacking in foresight. To these detractors, the controversial figure might appear to be causing unnecessary conflict, spreading misinformation or failing to consider the broader implications of their actions.

This dichotomy in perception is not just a matter of differing opinions but often reflects deeper divides within a society, be it cultural, political, ideological, or moral. The reasons behind such extreme reactions can be complex, involving a mix of personal values, social norms, historical context, and the influence of media portrayal.

Moreover, the tendency to categorise controversial figures in such binary terms overlooks the nuances of human behaviour and thought. Rarely do individuals fit neatly into the categories of a fool or a wise man. Their actions and beliefs can stem from a variety of motivations, intentions, and circumstances, many of which might not be immediately apparent to outside observers.

To navigate this complexity, it is beneficial for observers to approach controversial figures with empathy and critical thinking. Seeking to understand the context of their actions, the nuances of their arguments and the reasons behind their support or criticism can lead to a more nuanced and less polarised discourse. It encourages moving beyond simplistic labels and towards a deeper understanding of the multifaceted nature of human behaviour.

Being Helpful and Being Trusting

Being helpful is a powerful antidote to feelings of helplessness. When we extend a helping hand to others, we not only provide support and assistance but also empower ourselves. By actively engaging in acts of kindness and lending a helping hand, we break free from the shackles of helplessness and tap into our innate ability to make a positive difference in the lives of others.

Moreover, being helpful not only benefits us individually but also strengthens the fabric of our communities and society. When we come together and offer our skills, resources, and time to assist others, we create a culture of compassion and cooperation. This culture fosters a sense of belonging and unity, as we recognise that we are all interconnected and that our collective well-being depends on the well-being of others.

Similarly, being trusting allows us to build trustworthiness. When we trust others, we create an environment that encourages open communication, honesty, and mutual respect. Trust is a two-way street; by extending trust to others, we inspire them to trust us in return. This reciprocal trust forms the basis for meaningful connections, effective teamwork, and successful partnerships.

Being trustworthy is not just about being reliable and dependable; it is also about being authentic and genuine. When we consistently demonstrate trustworthiness through our actions and words, we earn the respect and confidence of those around us. Trustworthiness is a valuable trait that allows us to forge lasting relationships, inspire loyalty, and create a positive reputation.

In summary, being helpful and trusting are essential qualities that contribute to personal growth, community development and the overall well-being of society. By embracing these qualities, we can foster a culture of support, collaboration, and trust, leading to a more harmonious and prosperous world.

Trustworthy People Are Those Who Trust

Those who trust others are often seen as trustworthy themselves. Trust is a two-way street that can foster positive relationships and create a sense of mutual respect and reliability. When someone demonstrates trust in others, it can inspire confidence and encourage honesty and integrity in return. Trustworthiness is a valuable trait that can strengthen connections and build a foundation of trust in personal and professional interactions. It is a reminder of the power of trust in shaping our relationships and the way we are perceived by others.

In the world of business, successful deals often result from a win-win situation where all parties involved benefit and feel satisfied with the outcome. Trust, truth, and transparency play a crucial role in fostering such mutually-beneficial agreements.

Dad always said, *listen to everyone, but make your own decision.*

> The depth of ownership is profound,
>
> Responsibility and pride are tightly wound,
>
> In the sense of belonging, we are aligned,
>
> To produce with the art and craft so refined.

Belonging stirs, a fire within,
Igniting a passion for work to begin,
Responsibility takes its rightful place,
Guiding hands with steady grace.

Pride swells, a beacon bright,
In the darkest hours, a guiding light,
Reliability blooms from this sacred ground,
Where ownership and belonging are found.

In the journey of life's winding road,
Dad's lessons pave, a path bestowed.
With commitment and reliability as our creed,
In his wisdom, we find the strength we need.

First, listen to all voices in the discussion's fray,
Consider the pros and cons, then choose your way.
Collaborate beyond your thoughts, let ideas play,
In teamwork's embrace, fruitful discussions stay.

How Can You Be So Intolerant?

HIM: How can you be so intolerant?

ME: Because tolerance can be both, good and bad. For example, if I tolerate nonsense or addictive substances, it is wrong.

HIM: We are talking about your behaviour with good people you cannot stand. How can you be so heartless?

ME: Sorry! Let's focus on the importance of tolerance. It is crucial to know where to lower it and where to increase it. Tolerance is inversely proportional to ego, making it a valuable tool for navigating life's challenges.

HIM: When you understand yourself, you begin to understand others and become more tolerant of them.

ME: Tolerance can also have negative effects, particularly in the context of habit-forming substances and precision work.

HIM: Tolerance, as the capacity to accept and respect differences in opinions, beliefs, and behaviours, is a virtue that can greatly impact our lives.

ME: Lowering tolerance increases your capacity to fight addiction, whereas increasing tolerance makes you more flexible.

HIM: Flexibility is the art of increasing or decreasing your tolerance level at will. Increase it in toil or in a relationship and decrease it in your dependence.

ME: The battle of tolerance is a battle of wits in another form.

HIM: The ongoing curfew is a test of the tolerance of married couples.

ME: Despite the wider variety of animals and plants over humans, their tolerance for each other is far higher.

HIM: Unrestricted enjoyment is not readily tolerated.

ME: Accepting or tolerating demands logic to reap its benefits.

HIM: You can accept failure, but not defeat, also, you can increase your tolerance in a relation, but not with alcohol or addiction.

ME: Patience comes from tolerance of oneself which comes from acceptance of oneself.

HIM: The inherently tolerant people are probably the more vulnerable ones.

ME: Fundamentally tolerant people are likely to be vulnerable.

HIM: You can reduce your tolerance to the use of intoxicants and increase it to face life.

ME: When both sides of our minds learn to tolerate one another, we will be blissful.

HIM: Tolerance? Sounds like a fancy word for not getting into arguments all the time.

ME: It's more than that, buddy. Tolerance is about respecting others, even when we don't see eye to eye.

HIM: I get it. But let's be real, it's hard to stay calm when someone's pushing all your buttons.

ME: True, but that's where humility comes in. When we let go of our egos, we make room for understanding and compassion.

HIM: I guess you're right. So, how do we practice tolerance in our daily lives?

ME: By listening more, judging less, and approaching differences with an open mind. It's about building bridges, not walls.

HIM: Well, I'll drink to that! Understanding oneself? Sounds like a deep dive into the mind and soul.

ME: Absolutely. When we take the time to explore our own thoughts and emotions, we gain a deeper understanding of ourselves and others.

HIM: It's like peeling back the layers of an onion, revealing more about who we are and how we relate to the world around us.

ME: Exactly! Self-awareness is the key to empathy and compassion, allowing us to see the humanity in everyone we meet.

HIM: And when we approach others with tolerance and acceptance, we create a space for meaningful connections and harmonious relationships to flourish.

ME: That's the beauty of it. By embracing our own vulnerabilities and imperfections, we can relate to others with kindness and understanding.

HIM: So, let's raise a toast to self-discovery, empathy, and the power of tolerance in building a more inclusive and compassionate world for all.

ME: Cheers to that, my friend. Here's to embracing differences, fostering unity, and shining bright with the light of tolerance in our hearts.

Storytelling Should Mirror the Speed of Life

In today's fast-paced world, storytelling should adapt to keep up with the changing times. Just as our lives are moving at a rapid pace, our stories should also reflect the same level of excitement, engagement, and speediness. By embracing a dynamic and fast-paced storytelling style, we can capture the attention of modern audiences and keep them engaged throughout the narrative. This can be achieved through concise and impactful storytelling techniques, incorporating unexpected twists and turns, and using innovative mediums such as interactive storytelling or multimedia elements. Ultimately, by aligning our storytelling with the fast-paced nature of contemporary life, we can ensure that our stories resonate with and captivate audiences in this rapidly evolving world.

While personal experiences can certainly add depth and authenticity to storytelling, research also plays a crucial role in creating compelling narratives. Writing solely based on personal experiences may limit the scope and variety of stories that can be told. Research allows writers to explore different perspectives, cultures, and periods, expanding the richness and diversity of their storytelling. It helps to ensure accuracy, credibility, and a well-rounded understanding of the subject matter. By combining personal experiences with thorough research, writers can create narratives that are both relatable and informative, capturing the essence of the human experience while also providing valuable insights and knowledge.

A focused mind can illuminate the details, but an open mind reveals the hidden secrets.

Let us explore how a focused mind and an open mind can benefit a heat exchanger manufacturing company.

A focused mind within the context of a heat exchanger manufacturing company would involve paying close attention to the technical specifications, design details and manufacturing processes. Engineers and technicians would need to concentrate on the intricate components, materials and assembly techniques involved in creating efficient and reliable heat exchangers. By focussing on these details, the company can ensure the highest quality and performance of its products.

On the other hand, an open mind within the same context would involve being receptive to new ideas, innovations, and advancements in the field of heat exchanger technology. This could mean exploring alternative materials, novel designs or emerging manufacturing techniques that could enhance the efficiency, durability, or environmental sustainability of the heat exchangers. An open mind would also encourage collaboration and knowledge-sharing with other experts in the industry, enabling the company to stay at the forefront of new developments.

By combining a focused mind with an open mind, the heat exchanger manufacturing company can achieve excellence in both - the details and the broader industry landscape. They can produce high-quality products that meet the specific needs of their customers while staying adaptable and responsive to the evolving demands of the market. This approach would not only ensure the company's success but also foster a culture of continuous improvement and innovation within the organisation.

Unlike many other countries, India presents unique opportunities for vocational training and wellness centres to thrive due to its population growth and aging trends. Population growth in India has led to an expanding workforce and a large pool of young individuals seeking employment opportunities. This presents an opportunity for vocational training centres to play a crucial role in equipping the youth with the necessary skills and knowledge to meet the demands of the job market. By providing vocational training programs in sectors such as technology, healthcare, hospitality and manufacturing, these centres can help bridge the skills gap and enhance employability.

At the same time, India is also experiencing a significant demographic shift towards an aging population. This presents an opportunity for wellness centres to cater to the needs of older adults. Wellness centres can offer a range of services, including fitness programs, healthcare services, mental health support and social activities to promote active and healthy aging. With the increasing awareness and importance of holistic well-being, wellness centres can thrive by providing specialised care and services tailored to the needs of older individuals.

Both, vocational training, and wellness centres, can contribute to India's economic growth and social development. By investing in these sectors, the government, private organisations, and individuals can create employment opportunities, enhance productivity, and improve the overall quality of life for both, the younger and the older population.

Policymakers, businesses, and communities need to recognise and capitalise on these opportunities. By supporting the establishment and growth of vocational training and wellness centres, India can harness the potential of its population growth and aging trends, ultimately leading to a more prosperous and inclusive society.

Manufacturing Vs Filmmaking

Both, the manufacturing of tubular heat exchangers and filmmaking have a desperate need for revolutionary change. While on the one hand manufacturing suffers from high costs and low efficiencies because of performance failures, filmmaking is missing out on original content and fresh talent.

Reach

Both have an unlimited reach. Films and videos are seen in every corner of the globe by every segment of society and the entire range of demographics. Tubular heat exchangers are used by every process - exothermic or endothermic – to produce electrical energy from solar, thermal power and nuclear power plants. Even our bodies are heat exchangers; otherwise, how can our body temperature stay normal in the coldest or hottest conditions?

Variety

There is no limit to the variety of films. Everything that is shot in motion is a film, whether it is a child's fantasy, animation, sci-fi, documentary, advertising video, brand creation film, education, motivation, or anything else. This is also true of heat exchangers. Built to every shape and size, the diversity is as enormous as the purpose they serve.

Freedom of expression

Whether filmmaking or manufacturing, the set rules do not allow the germination of new ideas. Scriptwriters, directors, and editors are like licensors, EPCs and manufacturers respectively. Too many cooks spoil the broth. Moreover, a storyteller is an all-in-one who completes the film as an editor. Likewise, the tubular exchanger manufacturer satisfies the end-users needs from start to finish. Whether hardware or a film, creativity can come only from a solitary source.

Innovation

Implementation of new ideas is innovation. In manufacturing, we must transform the abstract into a prototype and go further by fabricating the equipment and creating a production history that functions well.

Crafting art is innovation. Narration with the camera is filmmaking. Connect your audience to visuals, not words, as body language conveys everything. Everyone inherently perceives this purity of body language that is acting. Each one of us is a born actor. How else can we survive in this wicked world?

Implementation

Finally, implementation is not an individual activity in manufacturing or moviemaking. Like-minded people get together to form a manufacturers' association. This body invites manufacturing outfits, professionals, and fellow entrepreneurs to voice their opinion on a win-win solution.

In moviemaking, we have the entire team, from the actors to the technicians, entirely at home with the storytelling. This can be done by conducting script workshops. These are visual script workshops with only the premise and structure. Keeping this in mind, the workshops draw on reality to make sure that every step moves towards the purpose of the premise.

All events are created on the spot; the participants' actions and reactions studied, and their performances examined. In short, it is about tracking the protagonist and the others with the camera. Editing is done by juxtaposing shots to make a scene, and scenes are joined together to make a movie. The story is straightforward.

Direction

Being the leader of the team, a director must be good in all aspects of filmmaking. He is the origin, the storyteller. A director must understand the person behind the actor to mould him into the character. To do so, he must be an actor first. A film as a product is organic only if the director is a storyteller. The story should be his own, otherwise, it is just show business. You talk to the audience, not at them. When a director makes a movie from a screenplay that is created from someone else's story, he is not the storyteller.

Storytelling

The art of storytelling comes from your nightmares, not from your dreams. The beauty of a script lies in storytelling, which is sensed and felt, without the barrier of language.

To be a storyteller, build your characters around the actors to make them real, and not mere reel images. Moviemaking is the art of telling a story through actors who have been moulded into the characters. Storytelling - not treatment - is the prime need.

Resource Planning in Designing and Filmmaking

Designing based on availability to reduce costs and meet immediate needs is much like producing a movie with consideration for actor and location availability. In both cases, success hinges on adaptability and resourcefulness.

In filmmaking, directors and producers often find themselves working within constraints - whether it is the schedule of a sought-after actor or the availability of a picturesque location. They must navigate these parameters to create a cohesive and engaging story. Similarly, in design, engineers and creators must work with the resources at hand, considering the materials, tools, and technologies available to them to develop efficient and cost-effective solutions.

Just as filmmakers creatively adjust their scripts and shooting schedules to make the most of available talent and settings, designers must harness their ingenuity to shape their concepts around what is readily accessible. This approach not only helps manage costs but also ensures that projects are completed on time to meet immediate demands.

Ultimately, both processes highlight the importance of strategic planning and adaptability, transforming limitations into opportunities that pave the way for innovation and success.

Using Familiar Locations in Storytelling

When you write with familiar locations in mind, you can bypass the need to search for matching settings, thereby avoiding confusion and other potential issues.

Writing with known and accessible locations can simplify the storytelling process and add a layer of authenticity and practicality to your narrative. By using familiar settings, you can avoid the logistical challenges and potential disconnect that come with trying to match story elements to unfamiliar places.

Using familiar locations not only simplifies the writing process but also enhances the believability and emotional resonance of your story. By drawing deeply from places, you know well, you can create rich, authentic settings that breathe life into your narrative and captivate your audience.

Instead of visualising the characters and choosing the actors to portray them, it is easier to pick the characters known to you for their reactions to the events to narrate your story at a much lower cost authentically.

Leveraging familiar characters from your life, who you know well and can accurately predict their reactions, can add a layer of authenticity and relatability to your story. Moreover, by adhering to their realistic and predictable behaviours, you create richer, more believable interactions and a story that feels genuine and engaging. This method not only grounds your narrative but also allows you to craft a compelling story cost-effectively.

The More Money You Make, The More Insecure You Become

The more money you make, the more insecurity you may feel, largely due to the pressures that come with maintaining and protecting that wealth. As your financial assets grow, so does the complexity of managing them, which can lead to stress and anxiety. Additionally, increased wealth can attract fair-weather friends - individuals who are more interested in what you can offer them materially rather than genuine companionship. This can make it difficult to trust others and form meaningful relationships.

However, if the accumulation of wealth is driven by a noble purpose, such as philanthropy or contributing to societal improvement, it can provide a sense of fulfilment and direction. This purpose-driven approach can counterbalance the negative aspects of wealth, offering clarity and a strong sense of personal values, which help in navigating the challenges that come with financial success.

Unlike Money, Prosperity Is Immeasurable

Prosperity encompasses a wide range of aspects in life that go beyond mere financial riches. It includes factors such as well-being, fulfilment, relationships, personal growth, and overall happiness. Prosperity is a holistic concept that cannot be quantified solely by money.

In today's fast-paced and materialistic world, the terms *wealth* and *money* are often used interchangeably. While money can certainly contribute to wealth, it is just one piece of the puzzle. Wealth encompasses a wide range of tangible and intangible assets that enrich our lives in ways that money alone cannot.

At its core, money is a medium of exchange, a tool for transactions and a measure of value. It enables us to acquire goods and services, invest in opportunities and secure our future. While money is essential for meeting our basic needs and achieving financial security, it is not the sole indicator of wealth.

Wealth, on the other hand, is a more holistic concept that includes not only financial resources but also intangible assets such as knowledge, skills, relationships, health, experiences, and values. These intangible assets contribute to our overall well-being, happiness, and fulfilment in life. Wealth can be seen as the abundance of resources that enrich our lives and enable us to thrive in all aspects of life.

One important aspect of wealth is the idea of *brand*, which encompasses one's reputation, influence, and impact on others. Building a strong personal brand involves cultivating a positive image, values and relationships that can open doors, create opportunities, and leave a legacy. A strong brand can be an asset that enhances one's wealth in ways that money alone cannot.

Furthermore, wealth can also be viewed as the *noble cause*, referring to the positive impact, contributions and service to others that define a person's legacy. Engaging in acts of kindness, generosity and philanthropy can create a sense of fulfilment and purpose that transcends material wealth. These assets in *God's bank* represent the goodwill, compassion, and positive influence that one accumulates through acts of service and selflessness. Contrary to this, money beyond needs is greed, which is the worst addiction. It makes rich trillionaires crave more by hook or crook, extorting money from businesses to fill their coffers and egos.

In conclusion, while money is an important tool for achieving financial security and meeting our needs, true wealth encompasses a broader definition of prosperity. By recognising the difference between wealth and money, we can strive for a more balanced and fulfilling life that goes beyond material riches to embrace the true essence of prosperity.

Wealth and money, are not one and the same,

True prosperity goes beyond the financial game.

From knowledge to kindness, a noble cause,

Enriching lives with true wealth's legacy.

A leader's wealth in inspiring change,
Empowering others on a path so strange.
Their influence, a legacy that shines bright,
Enriching lives with courage and might.

An engineer's wealth in building new ways,
Innovating solutions that brighten our days.
Their creations, a bridge to a future unknown,
Enriching lives with the progress they have sown.

An innovator's wealth in ideas that spark,
Revolutionising industries with a creative mark.
Their visions, a beacon of change and hope,
Enriching lives with possibilities to cope.

An entrepreneur's wealth in the risks they take,
Venturing into the unknown for innovation's sake.
Their ventures, a testament to courage and drive,
Enriching lives with opportunities to thrive.

Religion And Man

Are religions inherently diverse, or do we create distinctions between them?

Religions are different in their beliefs, practices, and traditions, but ultimately, they all aim to provide guidance, meaning and connection to something greater than ourselves. It is often the interpretations and practices of individuals within each religion that can make them seem different. At their core, many religions share common values such as love, compassion and understanding.

Why do we attribute all conflicts in the world to religion?

Religion can be a powerful force in shaping beliefs, values, and identities, which can sometimes lead to conflicts and differences among people. When individuals or groups strongly identify with their religious beliefs, they may view those who hold different beliefs as a threat or as *other*. This can lead to misunderstandings, prejudices and even violence. It is important to remember that at the heart of most religions are teachings of compassion, tolerance and understanding, and focusing on these common values can help bridge differences and promote harmony.

The most significant conflicts in history have often been religious in nature.

The Holy Wars, also known as the Crusades, were a series of religious wars fought between Christians and Muslims in the medieval period. These wars were fuelled by religious fervour, political ambitions, and economic interests. The Crusades had a significant impact on the history of Europe and the Middle East, leading to widespread violence, destruction, and loss of life. While the Holy Wars were indeed some of the largest and most devastating conflicts in history, it is important to recognise that wars have been fought for a variety of reasons, including political power, resources, and territorial disputes, not just religion.

Religion and the concept of God serve as tools to manipulate the emotions of vulnerable followers worldwide.

Religion and belief in God can indeed have a powerful influence on people's emotions and behaviours. For some, religion provides a sense of comfort, purpose, and community, while for others, it can be a source of division, conflict, and control. The interpretation and practice of religion can vary greatly among individuals and communities, leading to both positive and negative outcomes.

Ultimately, how religion is practiced and its impact on individuals and society depends on how it is interpreted, applied, and shared by its followers. People need to engage in thoughtful reflection and dialogue about the role of religion in their lives and in the world around them.

Civilisation is the foundation from which religion emerges.

The relationship between civilisation and religion is complex and multifaceted. While some scholars argue that religion is an integral part of human civilisation and has played a significant role in shaping societal norms, values and institutions, others suggest that religion has evolved alongside human civilisation to make sense of the world and address existential questions.

Throughout history, religion has been a central aspect of many civilisations, influencing art, architecture, governance, and social practices. Religious beliefs and rituals have often provided a sense of identity, community and moral guidance for individuals and societies.

At the same time, civilisations have also shaped the development and expression of religious beliefs. The interaction between culture, politics and religion has led to the diversity of religious traditions and practices seen around the world today.

Overall, the relationship between civilisation and religion is intricate and dynamic, with each influencing and being influenced by the other in various ways. It is a topic of ongoing study and debate among scholars and thinkers seeking to understand the complexities of human belief and behaviour.

Every religion places a strong emphasis on the value of humanity.

Indeed, the concept of humanity is a common thread that runs through many religions and spiritual beliefs around the world. While the specific teachings and practices may vary, the underlying message of compassion, kindness, empathy, and respect for all human beings is a central tenet in most faith traditions. This emphasis on humanity encourages followers to treat others with love, understanding and dignity, regardless of differences in beliefs, backgrounds, or circumstances. By promoting values such as generosity, forgiveness, tolerance and social justice, religions aim to foster harmonious relationships, build strong communities, and create a more compassionate and equitable society. Ultimately, the shared focus on humanity serves as a unifying force that transcends cultural boundaries and promotes the common good of all individuals, reinforcing the importance of empathy, solidarity, and care for one another in our shared human experience.

4. Self Help

Self-Acceptance

His Story

Once there was a man, wise but flawed,
Who found love in a girl, much less than half his age.
Their bond grew strong, though his guilt gnawed,
For societal norms cast a shadow on their stage.

Fifteen years they journeyed, hand in hand,
He did the world for her, but was it spoiling?
A married man with grandkids, he took a stand,
To make her independent, her dreams uncoiling.

Education and profession, he bestowed with care,
Yet trials and fallacies clouded their path.
She took it for granted, unaware,
Her guilt surfaced, bringing her family's wrath.

Time slipped away, as they strived and fought,
Her independence was a gift, but at what cost?
For now, she loves another, as she ought,
Leaving him heartbroken, his dreams lost.

In the end, he learnt a lesson profound,
Of self-acceptance and love's bittersweet sound.
For in letting go, true love is found,
Embracing flaws, on new beginnings he's bound.

When we embrace our flaws and strengths alike,
Our hearts open to others, shining bright.
Accepting oneself is the key,
To understand others, setting us free.

To truly see beyond the external guise,
We must look within, where the truth lies.
Acknowledging our fears and desires,
Paves the way for genuine connections to transpire.

Self-acceptance is the foundation,
On which empathy and compassion find their station.
Only when we love ourselves completely,
Can we extend that love unreservedly?
So let us start with ourselves, without delay,
For in self-acceptance, true acceptance will stay.
Embracing who we are, flaws and all,
Allows us to answer love's universal call.

Taking Hold of The Present

Taking hold of the present is about being fully engaged and mindful in the current moment. Here are a few steps to get you there.

Practice mindfulness: Mindfulness is the practice of being fully present and aware of your thoughts, feelings, and sensations in the present moment. It involves paying attention to your surroundings, your breath, and the sensations in your body. Engaging in mindfulness exercises such as meditation or deep breathing can help you cultivate a greater sense of presence.

Prioritise self-care: Taking care of your physical and mental well-being is crucial for being in the present. Make sure to get enough sleep, eat nutritious meals, exercise regularly and engage in activities that bring you joy and relaxation. When you prioritise self-care, you are better able to be fully present and engaged in the present moment.

Limit distractions: In today's digital age, distractions are abundant. To take hold of the present, it is important to minimise distractions as much as possible. Turn off notifications on your phone, create designated times for checking emails and social media, and create a calm and clutter-free environment that allows you to focus on the present moment.

Set goals and priorities: Having clear goals and priorities can help you stay focussed on the present. By setting specific, achievable goals, you can break them down into actionable steps and work on them one at a time. This helps you direct your energy and attention towards what matters in the present moment.

Practice gratitude: Cultivating a sense of gratitude for the present moment can help you appreciate and fully experience it. Take a moment each day to reflect on the things you are grateful for, whether it is the people in your life, the opportunities you have, or the simple pleasures that bring you joy. This practice can help shift your perspective and bring you into a state of presence and appreciation.

Taking hold of the present is a continuous practice. It requires conscious effort and a willingness to let go of distractions and worries about the past or future. By cultivating a present-focussed mindset, you can fully experience and make the most of each moment as it unfolds.

As the present takes hold, embracing the future becomes second nature. The present has a way of shaping our perspective and influencing our actions. In this fast-paced world, where change is constant and innovation is celebrated, it is only natural that our mindset becomes more forward-thinking and futuristic. We find ourselves drawn to the possibilities that lie ahead, eagerly embracing new technologies, ideas, and opportunities.

Being futuristic means having a mindset that is open to the potential of what is to come. It involves being proactive, adaptable, and willing to explore uncharted territories. It is about envisioning a future that is not limited by the constraints of the present, but rather fuelled by imagination and a desire for progress.

In a world that is constantly evolving, being futuristic allows us to stay ahead of the curve. It encourages us to seek out new solutions to current challenges and to anticipate future needs. It empowers us to think creatively, to push boundaries, and to find innovative ways to improve our lives and the world around us.

Embracing a futuristic mindset also means being aware of the impact our actions have on the future. It involves considering the long-term consequences of our choices and striving to make decisions that are sustainable, ethical, and beneficial for generations to come.

Ultimately, being futuristic is not just about being fascinated by the possibilities of tomorrow, but also about acting today to shape a better future. It is about being proactive, forward-thinking, and willing to embrace change. By doing so, we can contribute to a world that is constantly evolving and progressing, and leave a positive legacy for future generations.

Actions Are Misleading as They Are Not in Our Control

The statement that actions are misleading as they are not in our control raises an interesting philosophical question about the nature of human agency and free will. It suggests that our actions may not truly reflect our intentions or character because they are influenced by external factors beyond our control.

From a deterministic perspective, one could argue that all actions are predetermined by a chain of causality, whether it be biological, environmental, or societal. According to this view, our choices and actions are ultimately the result of prior causes and we are merely conduits for these forces. In this sense, one might say that actions can be misleading because they do not fully represent our true selves or intentions.

However, it is important to consider the complexity of human behaviour and the role of consciousness and decision-making in our actions. While external factors undoubtedly influence our choices, humans also possess a degree of agency and the ability to exercise free will. We can reflect, deliberate, and make conscious decisions based on our values, beliefs, and desires.

While it is true that external influences can shape our actions, it is also true that we have the power to resist or transcend these influences through self-awareness and self-control. We can choose to act in ways that align with our true intentions and values, even in the face of external pressures or circumstances.

In this light, actions can still be seen as meaningful and reflective of our character, even if they are influenced by external factors. While we may not have complete control over every aspect of our actions, we can still strive to act in ways that are consistent with our internal beliefs and values.

Ultimately, the question of whether actions are misleading or not is a complex and nuanced one. It requires a deeper exploration of the nature of human agency, free will and the interplay between internal intentions and external influences.

Freedom Is Merely a Mindset

Freedom is as difficult to define as love, happiness, or life in its entirety. You can break free of something and relate to something else. When you would rather be a boss than work under someone else's orders, would that set you free? No, on the contrary, you are going to be dependent on many instead of only one.

Will money give you freedom? No way! The more you make, the more you would want. You cannot run from life, even if you escape to the mountains.

So how to get there without giving up life? You can do it when you live on the edge. Freedom can only be attained from within. However, this journey is an enormous sacrifice, as nothing is free, and therefore not freedom, for sure. I remember something from my past that is a case in point.

It is about a brilliant, energetic, and good-looking boy with retarded growth. He was five foot nothing even at the age of twenty. The experts gave up hope as the growth plates were unresponsive. In every other way, he was par excellence. However, the inferiority complex led to overcompensation, as it had increased his strength and flexibility.

He could lead to greater heights and his muscular body had everything he needed to keep the toughest bullies of the university at bay. He was the captain of the cricket team, being the best batsman in the history of the university. He was one of the best students and often topped the class. While going to flashy parties, he would wear four-inch heels to shake the show with stylish dance moves and make the girls go after him.

One day he came across an adorable girl. He stood dumbstruck as she walked past without even noticing him. It was strange, no one on the campus had ever done this to him. Women were generally enchanted by him. He turned around to follow her and had to accelerate his steps to get to her stride. As he caught up with her, he was mesmerised but once again failed to get her attention. He then saw a man looking down at him yelling, "move away Shorty" as the man put his arms around the girl. The man was six feet two and the woman of his dreams was close to five feet nine. It was then that he realised his insignificance that could not reach their level. He almost collapsed at the thought with an overwhelming feeling of worthlessness.

He was madly in love, but he could not gather the courage to tell her because his self-esteem was low. He felt unworthy of her; she deserved someone much taller than him. He had been living in self-denial. There was a change in him as everyone noticed, his lack of interest was apparent in all his activities. Everyone was concerned because, without him, there was a vacuum. They wanted to get to the bottom of this noticeable change. They found out it was a girl, a second-year student in the faculty of Home Science. A docile and good-natured girl who was completely unaware of all the commotion she had caused. It was too personal a question for anyone to ask.

The boy resolved to disconnect from the world to free himself of the burden of trying to prove what he was not. He was short and so insignificant; he had to accept this and not live in self-denial. He remembered his dad singing his favourite song *Walk Tall* by Val Doonican with a part of its lyrics that kept resonating in his ears: *Be a proud man and hold your head up high, walk tall! Look the world right in the eye.*

This gave him the courage, a grit he had demonstrated quite well earlier, but now he had to face the truth. To be in love with someone much taller he did not deserve and yet nothing could stop him from loving her. He experienced a weird feeling, a realisation that he loved himself for loving her so deeply. This gave him confidence and the intention to achieve higher goals in life. Be a believer it is only you in you, nothing can influence you anymore, and you are independent. He was going to be free; the thoughts were reverberating strongly. He would continue with the good work he has been doing, no more flashy stuff, just helping others as he always did. He was now a freedom seeker.

Achieving independence is freedom,
And to attain dependability is wisdom.

Freedom to do what you want is an illusion,
Choosing to do so causes all the confusion.

Real freedom is when you have no choice.
As then the reasoning will have no voice.

Freedom is doing without thinking,
Without knowing and without reasoning.
Liberty signifies enslavement to faith,
It is when you surrender to your fate.

He got back in the saddle with much vigour, to everyone's relief. However, showing off at fancy parties and the 4-inch heels became things of the past. That is when he accepted himself, so to speak, living with himself, and not in denial. He was finally free, just like he surrendered to his destiny.

He was at peace with himself. The look on his face showed that he was freed from being an arrogant and boisterous person. Love made him see God in her and then in himself, which took him a long time to realise.

The memory of the sight is all he needed from time to time to assure him.

Sometime later, he was riding past the ladies' hostel when he noticed a man harassing a woman. He pressed the brakes on his scooter and turned back when he heard her scream. The man almost strangling her. He asked the man to stop but was beaten by the man who was tall and well built. He fell to the ground and rose immediately to deliver a hard kick on the man's face. The man fell with a loud thud. He told the woman to run to the shelter without noticing the she was looking at him gratefully. He felt light and happy. He had learnt control from the realisation that life was all about living on the edge and balance.

Life is nothing but conflicts you face now and then,

The challenge that brings out the best in women and men.

Conflicts always exist but we ignore and push them under the carpet,

Thereby depriving ourselves of learning, missing out on life's target.

When you face life and deal with conflicts, there is a lot you learn,

When pushed to the wall, you think out of the box, flourish and earn.

> Living life to the fullest needs mind and body coordination,
>
> Living on the edge is balancing life, which is nothing but meditation.

His love story with her dream girl had evolved and set him free. Freedom of love has no attachment. He was not possessive and therefore not enslaved. This may be termed a detached attachment.

Breaking Free

The term *fan following* originated with the *punkha* in British India, where the sahibs and memsahibs had servants to swing the handy *punkha* (fan) for ventilation in the hot Indian summer.

In a cultural context, this can be seen as a metaphor for the dynamics of celebrity and their followers or supporters. Just as the *punkha* was a source of comfort for the colonial elite, fan followings today reflect the admiration and loyalty that people show toward their favourite public figures, albeit in a more modern and widespread sense.

While the historical connection may not directly define the modern term *fan following*, it is certainly a creative way to consider the evolution of the concept of fans and their role in providing support or appreciation for those in the spotlight.

Just as *punkha* means fan, *pankh* means wings. To break free from the bondage of subservience, we must embrace our wings and soar. The phrase '*pankh lagake ud jana'* suggests a desire to rise above constraints and embrace one's true potential, akin to how wings allow a bird to soar.

This notion resonates with broader themes of empowerment and self-determination. Just as wings enable flight, breaking free from societal expectations or historical hierarchies can lead to personal and collective growth. It speaks to the aspiration for individuals to take control of their narratives and rise above previous limitations.

From Guilt to Self-Love: A Path to Freedom

The ego that stems from self-attachment, rather than self-love, can diminish through practicing gratitude. This ego often thrives on comparison, competition, and a constant need for validation. Practising gratitude is a powerful way to shift the focus away from the ego and towards a sense of contentment, humility, and connection with the world around us.

Practicing gratitude allows individuals to develop a mindset of appreciation for the present moment and recognize the blessings in their lives. This shift in perspective can help diminish the ego's hold by fostering a sense of abundance, interconnectedness and joy that comes from recognising and acknowledging the good things in life. Gratitude can be a transformative practice that not only reduces the influence of the ego but also nurtures a deeper sense of self-love, compassion, and fulfilment.

Guilt often arises from a lack of self-love or self-awareness. When individuals don't have a deep sense of self-compassion or understanding of their thoughts, feelings, and motivations, they may be more prone to experiencing guilt in response to their actions or perceived shortcomings. Cultivating self-love and self-awareness can help individuals navigate their emotions, acknowledge their mistakes without harsh self-judgment, and ultimately work towards healing and growth. By fostering a strong sense of self-love and developing self-awareness, individuals can transform their relationship with guilt and move towards a more positive and empowering mindset.

Guilt is an emotional response to a real or perceived wrongdoing, where individuals feel remorse or regret for their actions or inactions. While the triggers and manifestations of guilt may vary from person to person, the root cause often stems from a sense of moral conflict, violated values or a belief that one has fallen short of their own expectations or societal norms.

The journey from guilt to self-love involves several important steps: awareness, acknowledgement, tolerance, acceptance, and self-love. By following these steps, individuals can navigate their feelings of guilt, understand them, and ultimately find self-compassion and acceptance. This process can lead to healing and growth, fostering a more positive and fulfilling relationship with oneself and others.

First comes awareness, then acknowledgement, followed by tolerance, then acceptance, and finally, self-love. This encapsulates a powerful progression of personal growth and self-discovery. Starting with awareness, the journey towards self-love unfolds through a series of transformative stages that require introspection, reflection, and emotional resilience.

Awareness marks the initial step, where one becomes conscious of their thoughts, emotions, and behaviours, laying the foundation for self-exploration and understanding. Acknowledgement follows, allowing individuals to confront their strengths, weaknesses and vulnerabilities with honesty and courage, paving the way for introspective growth and self-awareness.

Tolerance comes next, embodying the capacity to embrace imperfections, uncertainties and challenges with compassion and patience. It signifies a shift towards self-compassion and acceptance of one's experiences, flaws, and limitations, fostering inner peace and emotional resilience.

Acceptance represents a significant milestone in the journey towards self-love, signifying a deep sense of embracing oneself fully, without judgment or conditions. It involves coming to terms with one is past, present, and future, honouring personal truths, and acknowledging the beauty and complexity of one's authentic self.

Finally, self-love culminates in a profound sense of compassion, respect, and kindness towards oneself, nurturing a strong foundation of self-worth and inner healing. It encompasses self-care, self-empowerment, and self-affirmation, fostering a deep connection with one's essence and fostering a sense of wholeness and fulfilment.

This progression from awareness to self-love is a transformative and empowering journey, reflecting the profound growth and resilience that can be cultivated through self-reflection, acceptance and nurturing self-compassion. It emphasises the importance of embracing one's unique journey towards self-discovery and self-love, celebrating the beauty and strength that lie within each individual.

Freedom is guilt-free! Or is it the other way around? Freedom is indeed guilt-free, as it grants individuals the ability to make choices and act according to their beliefs and desires without feeling burdened by guilt. When one has the freedom to make choices and live authentically, it can lead to a sense of empowerment and fulfilment rather than guilt or shame.

On the other hand, feeling guilt-free can also be a form of freedom, as it allows one to move past negative emotions and experiences to embrace a more positive, liberated state of being. Ultimately, the relationship between freedom and guilt is complex and can vary depending on individual perspectives and experiences.

This journey from guilt to self-love and freedom is a profound and transformative process that requires introspection, self-compassion, and a willingness to let go of limiting beliefs and negative emotions. It is through this journey that individuals can find healing, growth, and a deep sense of connection with themselves and the world around them. Embracing self-love and freedom can lead to a life filled with joy, fulfilment, and inner peace.

Love Yourself for God's Sake

She: Harry! You keep telling me to love myself and I do exactly that.

Me: Is that so? That's nice!

She: No, it's terrible!

Me: Why?

She: They call me selfish.

Me: You don't love yourself. If you did, you wouldn't be telling me what others call you.

She: Why not?

Me: Because you wouldn't care. When you are in love with yourself, it doesn't matter what others think or say about you. You don't ask for their approval.

She: What do I do?

Me: Just cool down, it's not easy to love yourself. Most of us can't do it in our lifetime.

She: Then why do you tell me to do it? And make a fool of myself.

Me: The awareness is good enough, to achieve it is a far cry.

She: Tell me more.

Me: Be with yourself even when you are with others, be within! Try to be aware of yourself first, then understand yourself. Wait! No, it's not easy, we don't understand ourselves, we only understand as we're perceived. We are different from how we're perceived.

She: So, what must I do?

Me: It will take time, don't be hard on yourself, and don't mind being different from how you should be. Because how you think is how you have been made to think.

She: I guess so. I sometimes want to do something I dare not. Do you mean I should?

Me: Wait! Hear me out. Don't do anything, but the good part is you are aware of something. Just tolerate it to further your awareness, and a time will come when you will become aware of the unwanted self.

She: Oh my God!

Me: Yes indeed! The awareness comes, but acceptance of this will need faith in the God within.

She: What about loving myself?

Me: Self-acceptance will lead to self-love and not self-attachment, which causes selfishness.

She: And…?

Me: With self-love, you are selfless. You love everyone, and everyone reciprocates. You are at one with the God within, others will feel that in you, and you will feel that too by seeing them differently from how they're perceived by others.

She: Meaning?

Me: When you lower your guard to reveal your divine self, others are obliged to do the same, compelled by the laws of nature.

She: Oh! So much to do?

Me: Nothing to do, just accept and believe, and take as much time as it takes. There will be ups and downs. Enjoy the process!

Love Yourself For God's Sake

Love yourself for God's sake,
The worldly ethics are fake.
Go by the morals your love defines,
In your heart, the truth shines.

In a world filled with noise and false pretence,
It's easy to lose sight of our inner sense.
But deep within, a voice whispers clear,
Love yourself for God's sake, let your morals steer.

Society may dictate what's right or wrong,
But it's your love that makes you strong.
Listen to the voice that speaks from within,
Follow the morals that your heart has been given.

Love yourself for God's sake,
The worldly ethics are fake.
Go by the morals your love defines,
In your heart, the truth shines.

In self-love, you'll find the divine,
A connection that transcends space and time.
Let go of the judgments, the expectations imposed,
And embrace the morals that your love has composed.

So, love yourself deeply, with all your might,

In doing so, you align with the light.

Let your love guide you, let your morals be clear,

And live a life that's authentic, without fear.

Love yourself for God's sake,

The worldly ethics are fake.

Go by the morals your love defines,

In your heart, the truth shines.

Buckle Up or Buckle Under

What is good for travel is good for life as life is a journey. The phrase *buckle up* is used metaphorically to mean preparing or getting ready for challenges, while *buckle under* implies succumbing to pressure or difficulties.

The idea that life is a journey is a common metaphorical concept that highlights the similarities between life and travel. Just as in travel, life is filled with adventures, detours, challenges, and unexpected experiences. It emphasises the importance of enjoying the process, learning from different paths taken and adapting to changes along the way. Viewing life as a journey can provide perspective, encourage personal growth, and help individuals navigate through the ups and downs that come their way. It is a reminder to savour the moments and make the most of the ride, wherever it may lead. Expanding on the concept that "in life, if you don't buckle up, you're likely to buckle under" suggests that preparation and resilience are key factors in facing the challenges and pressures that life presents.

When you buckle up in life, you take the necessary steps to equip yourself with the skills, mindset and resources needed to navigate obstacles and unexpected circumstances. This can include setting goals, acquiring knowledge, building a support network, and cultivating a positive attitude.

On the other hand, if you fail to buckle up and prepare yourself adequately, you may find yourself overwhelmed by the demands and difficulties that come your way, leading to a sense of being unable to cope or buckling under the pressure.

By recognising the importance of readiness and resilience, you can better position yourself to handle life's challenges with strength, adaptability, and determination, ultimately allowing you to thrive and grow through whatever journey life may take you on.

Finding Balance: The Bottle v The Ball

In the fast-paced world of heavy engineering projects, where the pressure is high and the stakes higher, finding outlets for stress relief is essential. At Tema India, we understand the importance of supporting our team members in maintaining their well-being amidst challenging projects. As I reflected on ways to provide avenues for stress relief, I found myself drawn to two simple yet profound symbols: the bottle and the ball.

In the choice between lifting the bottle and hitting the ball, we are faced with a crucial decision that goes beyond mere physical actions. The bottle represents the spirit, not just in the form of alcohol but as a metaphor for seeking solace in temporary escapes. It offers a fleeting respite from the demands of our daily lives, a way to drown worries and momentarily find comfort. On the other hand, the ball embodies the sportsman spirit - discipline, dedication, teamwork, and the pursuit of a healthier lifestyle. It symbolises the commitment to excellence through physical activity and the drive to push oneself to new heights.

As we navigate the complexities of our work at Tema India, it is essential to consider the implications of our choices beyond the surface level. The decisions we make, whether to reach for the bottle or pick up the ball, can influence not only our well-being but also the collective spirit of our team. By embracing the values of discipline, teamwork and commitment exemplified by the ball, we can foster a culture of resilience and excellence within our organisation.

This juxtaposition of the bottle and the ball serves as a reminder that balance is key in all aspects of life - finding the equilibrium between moments of relaxation and periods of focused effort. By recognising the significance of both symbols in our pursuit of stress relief, we can strive to maintain harmony and productivity in our professional endeavours. Let us choose wisely, lift the ball with vigour, and propel ourselves towards a brighter, more fulfilling future.

The Ballad of Resilience: My Journey Through Betrayal and Triumph

Over 45 years ago, I had the pleasure of working with a talented chemical engineer named Nandu Bhide. With a shared passion for innovation, we collaborated on a project to refine dirty lube oil. Our excitement bubbled as we brainstormed solutions to simplify the process and reduce costs significantly. However, the journey took an unexpected turn when Nandu chose to align with a major corporation, leaving me feeling betrayed.

Amid shock and disappointment, I made a conscious choice to shift my focus from the hurt to something constructive. Instead of reaching for the bottle, I decided to hit the ball – finding solace and strength in sports and creativity.

This experience strengthened me to handle several more severe situations from time to time. And here is the song

I have composed to capture this journey. Thank you for your support as I navigate these challenges and emerge stronger on the other side.

As a part of this journey, I must mention that I fulfilled my desire to fly a plane by obtaining my Private Pilot License on a Cessna and also learned to sail.

Lift the bottle or the ball,

Think before you take a call.

Drink your way to drown your worries,

Hit the ball to take out your flurries

When betrayal strikes, confidence looms,

To avoid despair, seek support that resumes.

From the bottle, find solace, let joy be bloomed,

Hit the ball, feel your spirit zoom.

Nandu Bhide, a chemical engineer,

From Purdue he hails, his path is clear.

Faced with the choice, he knows it well,

One path to heaven, the other to hell.

From the bottle to the ball, choices before you stall,

Ponder well before deciding, don't let opportunities fall.

Drown worries with a sip, let your mind be light and airy,

Release frustrations with a swing, hit the ball, don't tarry.

True Learning Comes with Pain and Relief

You may read and reproduce knowledge, but true learning comes with both, pain, and relief. The path to understanding is often marked by moments of struggle, doubt, and frustration. These challenging experiences are integral to the learning process, pushing us beyond our comfort zones and encouraging growth.

However, with perseverance and effort, this journey also brings moments of clarity, insight, and satisfaction. The relief and joy that come with overcoming obstacles and achieving a deeper comprehension are invaluable. It is the blend of these challenging and rewarding experiences that enriches our minds and transforms mere information into meaningful knowledge.

Embracing both pain and relief inherent in learning allows us to develop resilience, adaptability, and a lifelong passion for personal and intellectual growth.

Negative Thoughts Serve a Positive Purpose

Negative thoughts, despite their connotation, can play a beneficial role in shedding light on potential disadvantages or drawbacks that may not have been immediately apparent. By embracing and exploring these negative thoughts, one can uncover valuable insights and perspectives that contribute to a more comprehensive understanding of a situation or idea. In essence, acknowledging and examining negative thoughts can lead to a more well-rounded and informed decision-making process.

A person holding such thoughts can be described as someone who values critical thinking and introspection, and seeks to understand different perspectives and uncover hidden insights. Such a person is open to exploring both, positive and negative aspects of situations, recognising that each holds valuable information that can contribute to the decision-making process. This individual is likely thoughtful, analytical, and open-minded, willing to challenge assumptions and delve deeper into complex issues.

Monotasking Or Multitasking

When you focus on one task at a time, you may tend to overdo it in pursuit of perfection, leading to a messy outcome due to anxiety.

The idea of one thing at a time may not always be as wise as it seems, as the pressure to achieve perfection can result in increased anxiety and a less-than-ideal result.

When you dedicate your attention solely to one task, there is a tendency to hyper-focus on every detail to achieve perfection. This intense focus can lead to heightened stress and anxiety as you strive to meet exceedingly high standards.

Consequently, this pressure to excel may paradoxically result in a counterproductive outcome, where the fear of making mistakes or falling short of perfection can lead to a chaotic and disorganised final product. It is essential to strike a balance between thoroughness and efficiency, acknowledging that perfection is not always attainable and that it is okay to embrace imperfections as part of the creative process.

Engaging in one task at a time can feel monotonous and limiting, especially when there is a desire for variety and excitement in our activities. The AI's perfectionist tendencies, while admirable in their pursuit of excellence, may inadvertently create a sense of being left out or unable to keep up with the fast-paced world around us. This dynamic can lead to a feeling of disconnect or a struggle to adapt to the ever-changing demands of our environment.

However, embracing a more flexible approach that allows for multitasking or switching between different activities can inject variety and dynamism into your workflow. This can help prevent boredom and keep things engaging while still maintaining productivity. Remember, it is okay to embrace imperfection and enjoy the process of learning and exploring new ways of doing things.

Life

Me: Life is like a complex puzzle, with each piece representing a different experience or emotion. It's fascinating how our perspectives can vary so widely, isn't it?

Him: Absolutely, it's like we're all looking at the same painting but interpreting it in our unique ways.

Me: Exactly! And that's the beauty of life - the diversity of thoughts and opinions that shape our understanding of the world.

Him: It's like a never-ending journey of self-discovery and growth.

Me: Absolutely, and embracing that journey with an open mind and a positive attitude can lead to a fulfilling and enriching life.

Him: Well said! It's all about finding joy in the little things and staying true to ourselves along the way.

Me: Indeed! Happiness is a choice we make every day, and it's up to us to create a life that brings us joy and fulfilment.

Him: Wise words! It's a reminder that life is what we make of it, and finding happiness within ourselves is the key to unlocking its true potential.

Me: Couldn't have said it better myself. Life is a canvas, and it's up to us to paint it with the colours of happiness and contentment.

Live For What Inspires You To Live

The longing for longevity motivates you to strengthen your muscles. Living for what inspires you can be a powerful motivator, not just mentally and emotionally, but physically as well. When you have a deep, intrinsic motivation, it often drives you to take better care of yourself, including strengthening your body. The following are some pointers on how to align your physical wellbeing with your passions and aspirations.

1. Connect physical activity to your passion

Incorporate what you love: If you are passionate about filmmaking, for instance, find ways to incorporate physical activity into your creative process. Maybe it is hiking to find the perfect filming location or taking dance classes to learn choreographic techniques.

Find enjoyable exercises: Choose physical activities that you genuinely enjoy. This can be anything from yoga and running to martial arts or swimming. The key is to find something that inspires you to stay active.

2. Set health and fitness goals

Personal milestones: Set specific, measurable, achievable, relevant and time-bound (SMART) goals related to your physical health. For example, aim to run a certain distance, lift a certain weight, or attend a specific number of workout sessions each week.

Health benchmarks: Track improvements in your physical health, such as increased energy levels, better sleep, and improved mood, all of which can directly enhance your capacity to pursue your passions.

3. Create a balanced routine

Holistic approach: Balance physical activities with your creative and professional work. Ensure you have a mix of cardio, strength training, flexibility exercises and plenty of rest. Consistent schedule: Establish a regular workout schedule that fits into your daily routine without conflicting with your other activities. Consistency is key to seeing long-term benefits.

4. Mind and body connection

Mindfulness practices: Engage in activities such as meditation or breathing exercises that help you stay present and focused. This can improve both your mental and physical health.

Yoga and stretching: Practices like yoga can help you maintain flexibility, reduce stress, and improve your overall well-being, all of which are beneficial for staying motivated and creative.

5. Healthy nutrition

Balanced diet: Fuel your body with a balanced diet that includes plenty of fruits, vegetables, lean proteins, and whole grains. Good nutrition supports physical health and mental clarity.

Stay hydrated: Drinking enough water each day is crucial for maintaining energy and focus.

6. Reward and reflect

Celebrate achievements: Celebrate your physical fitness achievements, no matter how small. Rewards can be a great motivator.

Reflect on progress: Regularly reflect on how improving your physical health has helped you in pursuing your passions. This reflection can reinforce your motivation.

7. Create a supportive network

Workout buddies: Find friends or join groups with similar fitness goals to keep each other motivated. A supportive network can provide accountability and encouragement.

Professional guidance: Consider seeking advice from fitness trainers or nutritionists to tailor a program that best fits your needs and goals.

Taking care of your physical health is an investment in your ability to live fully and passionately. By prioritising fitness, you are not only building a stronger body but also a stronger mind, allowing you to pursue what inspires you with greater vigour and resilience. Keep striving, stay motivated, and live for what truly inspires you.

Anything That Keeps You Working Is Good

Good or bad, anything that keeps you working is beneficial. However, if something hinders your ability to work, it is detrimental. The key lies in understanding and managing what motivates or obstructs your productivity.

Staying engaged and productive leads to growth, achievement, and the satisfaction of progress. Whether a conducive environment, supportive relationships or intrinsic motivation, such positive influences drive you forward. On the other hand, distractions, negative habits, or obstacles that impede your work can be harmful. They not only disrupt your workflow but also diminish your potential for success.

When you love what you do and do what you love, retirement may not even feel like a necessity. Some people find so much fulfilment and joy in their work that they choose to continue working well into their later years. For them, retirement might not be a specific event but rather a gradual transition or a change in focus. As long as you can continue doing what you love and it brings you happiness and fulfilment, there may be no need to retire in the traditional sense. It is all about finding that balance between work, passion, and personal well-being.

You do not retire when you love what you do and do what you love; instead, you retire when you are no longer able to pursue your passions, hopefully, when you are no more. In such a scenario, breaks are not sought, rather, avoided, unless it is a working holiday.

Recognising these dynamics allows you to cultivate a productive atmosphere and maintain focus, ensuring that you stay on the path to your goals.

Balancing The Mind for A Well-Deserved Sleep

When you take the time to balance your mind, you create a sense of harmony and peace within yourself. This inner balance allows you to let go of stress, worries and distractions, making it easier to relax and fall asleep at night. By practicing mindfulness, meditation, or other calming techniques, you can quieten your mind, release tension, and prepare yourself for a restful night's sleep. Prioritising mental balance not only improves the quality of your sleep but also enhances your overall well-being and resilience in facing life's challenges.

5. Machines, Technology, AI, And the Corporate World

Are We Machines?

Why else are we programmed? The education system and the work culture have put us in separate slots. Why are we not given the liberty to do as we please? You rather be a jack of all trades than a master of one. Specialisation kills human instincts while flexibility drives them. People in extreme situations become far-sighted. Like crafting the art of moviemaking can be better done using an engineer's logic and its creative side can be applied to innovate. A technocrat may also be a poet and vice versa. Otherwise, how do we develop all the learning functionalities?

What about the education system? I will draw on my experience at the MS University Baroda in the early 1960s. You will be surprised at what was taught to us: *Arrows should be narrow, and the lines should be fine, these are the principles of machine drawing.* No kidding! It was repeated from time to time and embedded in our brains. This was the time when the log and antilog tables were computing standards for every engineer to carry along with a T-square for drafting. A little later, the slide rule came along and then came the calculators. Now, we have smartphones and smartwatches to do anything we want.

During the five-year integrated engineering course, the advancement of technology progressed from log tables to a computer housed in a huge compartment. Does advanced computing define education? All this knowledge acquired became redundant shortly after graduation as computer-aided design calculations and drawings were first performed by a company called Tema India. No more blueprints and engineers busting their heads over each other.

Today, machinery does everything from design to construction. Also, read and compose and you just look and listen. There is no need for us to read or reproduce what is already abundant. Rather, enjoy doing what you like to do with no regulations. There is no point in competing against the machines to achieve perfection. Allow AI to deliver speed and perfection. We should be proud of human errors and imperfections where true beauty resides. When you attach yourself to a perfect partner, keep in mind that perfection is deliberate, and purity lies with the imperfect and the unbiased. Perfection is good for the camera, and not for the visionaries, who can look beyond.

The unfortunate thing is that over the years we have been programmed as machines. Our minds have been controlled by operators as in the case of machines. We were split to be governed by them. Everything we do has to be worthy of them. We are under the mundane pressure of running a rat race!

Will AI replace humankind? Yes, flawlessly! The machines are fast and without error. They can be programmed to capture the mind of every intellect and hue of an artist. However, they are not able to develop an EQ. The machines may come close, but not close enough to sense your feelings. Machines do not eat, drink, or delight. We should do this. Let us make the most of machines to do our dirty, inhuman work. We are creators, not machines. We are not aware of our potential because it cannot be quantified as with machines. We know the machines since we created them. A machine cannot replace its creator and neither can we.

Enhancing Performance Through Collaborative Design and Optimal Manufacturing

In the competitive landscape of global manufacturing, the key to creating successful products lies in the synergy between designers, manufacturers, and end users. At Tema India, we pride ourselves on going the extra mile to evaluate the performance of our equipment worldwide, even beyond its guarantee period. This commitment to continuous improvement serves as the foundation for our design enhancements and innovation.

A crucial aspect of product development is the close collaboration between designers and manufacturers. By tapping into the manufacturer's expertise in materials behaviour and production processes, designers can make informed decisions that elevate the quality and functionality of the final product. This partnership ensures that every aspect of the design is optimised for performance and durability, setting the stage for success in the market.

Moreover, involving end users in the design process is essential for understanding their performance expectations. By gathering feedback and insights, designers can tailor the product to meet specific user needs and preferences, resulting in a more user-centric design that enhances usability and market acceptance. This customer-focused approach not only improves the product's functionality but also fosters a deeper connection with the target audience.

In parallel, developing an optimal manufacturing sequence is paramount to streamlining production processes and enhancing performance for end users. By meticulously crafting efficient manufacturing workflows, manufacturers can reduce production timelines, improve user-friendliness during manufacturing, and ultimately deliver a superior product to the market. This strategic optimization not only accelerates production but also ensures a seamless and intuitive manufacturing experience for all stakeholders involved.

The benefits of an optimized manufacturing sequence extend beyond efficiency, as they directly impact the performance and functionality of the product. By fine-tuning the manufacturing process, manufacturers can deliver equipment that not only meets technical requirements but also exceeds user expectations. This focus on performance enhancement translates into higher levels of customer satisfaction, loyalty, and market success.

In conclusion, the collaborative efforts of designers, manufacturers, and end-users, coupled with an optimised manufacturing sequence, are essential pillars to creating high-performance products that resonate with global audiences. By embracing a holistic approach to design and manufacturing, companies can drive innovation, enhance user experiences, and stay ahead in today's competitive marketplace.

A New Approach to Designing

Going beyond manufacturing drawings

Designers should not confine their creativity and expertise to merely reading manufacturing drawings. While these drawings provide essential technical information, true innovation occurs when designers actively engage with the design process. They should proactively identify potential shortcomings and explore ways to enhance the design - whether that means improving functionality, optimising materials, or streamlining manufacturing processes.

This approach involves a comprehensive understanding of not just the aesthetics or mechanical viability of a product, but also the real-world challenges it might face during production and use. By stepping outside the confines of existing drawings, designers can anticipate issues that may not be apparent on paper, such as user experience, maintenance needs or sustainability concerns.

Furthermore, collaboration and feedback from cross-functional teams - engineers, marketers, and end-users - can often illuminate areas for improvement that a designer might not consider in isolation. This iterative design process fosters a culture of continuous improvement, where designs are regularly refined and modified based on testing, feedback and evolving market needs.

Ultimately, by embracing a mindset of adaptability and innovation, designers can create products that not only meet initial specifications but also exceed user expectations and contribute to a more efficient, sustainable, and impactful future.

Blueprints – a thing of the past

Gone are the days when people solely relied on blueprints to understand a product's design and functionality. The evolution of technology has transformed how we visualise products, making it possible to explore them in dynamic and interactive ways. Today, animations - buttoned and unbuttoned - offer a vibrant and engaging alternative to traditional blueprints.

These animations not only convey complex information more intuitively but also allow designers, engineers, and stakeholders to interact with the product virtually, observing how different components work together in real-time. Buttoned animations simulate the product's functions and features, providing insight into how users will engage with it, while unbuttoned animations can showcase the underlying mechanics, allowing for a deeper understanding of the design's intricacies.

This shift from static images to dynamic models enhances collaboration, enabling teams to visualise changes instantly and adjust designs on the fly. It fosters an environment of creativity and experimentation, where ideas can evolve rapidly without the constraints imposed by traditional methods. Stakeholders can also engage with these visual representations, providing feedback and input throughout the design process - thus promoting a more inclusive approach to product development.

Moreover, these advanced visualisation techniques not only boost efficiency and clarity during the design phase but also play a crucial role in marketing the product. High-quality animations can capture the attention of potential customers, showcasing the product's unique features and benefits in a way that static images alone cannot.

As we step into an era where visual storytelling becomes increasingly vital, utilising animations opens exciting new possibilities for how we design, visualise, and communicate about products. This shift enhances understanding and ultimately leads to the creation of better products that meet the evolving needs of users.

Assessing performance by analysing animations

Engineers can now assess performance by analysing animations through the lens of their critical practical experience. This modern approach enables a deeper understanding of how products function in real-world scenarios, going beyond traditional design reviews. By studying dynamic visualizations, engineers can observe intricate interactions among components, identify potential performance bottlenecks, and evaluate the overall functionality of a design before physical prototypes are created.

Visualising products in motion allows engineers to simulate various operating conditions, which helps in anticipating how the product will perform under stress, wear or during user interaction. Their practical experience informs this proactive analysis - engineers can draw on their knowledge of materials, mechanics, and user behaviour to critically evaluate animations, identifying both strengths and weaknesses in the design.

Moreover, this method enhances collaboration among multidisciplinary teams. Engineers can use animated simulations as a common reference point, facilitating discussions and feedback with designers, marketers, and stakeholders. This collaborative environment fosters innovation, enabling teams to iterate on designs quickly based on insights gained from performance analysis.

By leveraging animations and coupling them with their expertise, engineers can make informed decisions, leading to more robust designs that meet performance criteria and enhance user satisfaction. This evolution in evaluating product performance signifies a major advancement in engineering practices, ultimately contributing to the development of high-quality, reliable products.

Embracing AI In Engineering: The Need for Creative Thinking and Innovation

In the field of engineering, the integration of Artificial Intelligence (AI) has revolutionised traditional practices, reshaping the way professionals approach design, analysis and problem-solving.

AI offers capabilities such as predictive modelling, optimisation algorithms and data analysis that have transformed the way tasks are executed. From streamlining design processes to enhancing decision-making, AI has significantly improved efficiency and accuracy in engineering practices. However, as AI continues to evolve and expand its influence, engineers must embrace a mindset of creativity and innovation to unlock new possibilities and push the boundaries of what is achievable.

One of the key challenges facing engineers in the era of AI is the risk of becoming overly reliant on existing AI tools and methodologies, limiting the scope of problem-solving and innovation. To break free from this constraint, engineers must cultivate a culture of out-of-the-box thinking that encourages experimentation, exploration, and unconventional approaches to problem-solving. By embracing creativity and pushing beyond the boundaries of traditional AI applications, engineers can discover novel solutions, optimise processes, and drive meaningful advancements in their respective fields.

Moreover, the integration of AI in engineering presents an opportunity for professionals to collaborate across disciplines and industries, fostering a culture of knowledge exchange. By engaging with experts from diverse backgrounds and leveraging AI as a common language, engineers can gain fresh perspectives, spark innovative ideas, and co-create solutions that transcend conventional boundaries. This collaborative approach not only enriches the engineering practice but also cultivates a culture of continuous learning and growth.

In conclusion, while AI has become an indispensable tool in modern engineering, its true potential can only be realised through a combination of technical expertise, creative thinking, and a willingness to think outside the box. By embracing AI as a catalyst for innovation and adopting a mindset of exploration and experimentation, engineers can harness its power to drive transformative change, solve complex challenges and shape the future of engineering in unprecedented ways.

The Reliability Factor

Introducing the formula:

Reliability Factor (RF) = Deliveries Made (DM)/Commitments Taken (CT)

This formula represents a way to calculate the Reliability Factor based on the ratio of deliveries made to commitments taken.

This ratio is a valuable metric to evaluate reliability and accountability. By calculating this ratio, you can assess how well you follow through on your promises and obligations. A high ratio indicates a strong track record of reliability and integrity, while a low ratio may suggest a tendency to overcommit or struggle to fulfil obligations.

In the domain of commitments, a lesson so dear,

My dad's words echo, loud and crystal clear.

Commitments met, not a moment late,

Reliability is the key, a trait so great.

Introducing a metric, the Reliability Factor,

A formula to measure, a valuable actor.

> Deliveries made, commitments taken,
> A ratio to track, a promise unshaken.
>
> Proudly I stand, as my son leads the way,
> CEO with an RF of 0.85, come what may.
> Inspiring others, to reach even higher,
> In the pursuit of excellence, fuelling the fire.

This formula could be a useful tool for self-assessment, performance evaluation or goal setting, as it provides a numeric representation of reliability. By tracking and improving this Reliability Factor over time, individuals and organisations can prioritise effectively, manage workload efficiently, enhance their reputation, build trust with others, and achieve greater success in their endeavours.

Abstract To Proof: Creativity To Realisation

The path from abstract to proof is akin to a journey from creativity to realisation, filled with exploration and discovery. This process transforms innovative ideas into tangible solutions, enabling engineers and creators to bring their visions to life. It often begins with a spark of creativity - imaginative thoughts that challenge conventional boundaries and envision new possibilities.

As one navigates this journey, it fosters a sense of curiosity and encourages experimentation. The process of justifying each step along the way can be both fun and satisfying. It allows individuals to think critically, and assess various approaches and methodologies that contribute to the outcome.

Through meticulous reasoning and empirical testing, the initial abstract concepts are refined and solidified. Each iteration brings valuable insights, enhancing the understanding and leading to more robust solutions. The integration of creativity with technical rigour not only enriches the final product but also instils a deep sense of accomplishment.

Ultimately, this journey from abstract to proof embodies the joy of innovation, where ideas are transformed into reality, proving that creativity and practicality can go hand in hand. Moving from abstract ideas to concrete proof is akin to building castles in the air and bringing them to solid ground.

Initially, the imagination soars with limitless possibilities, constructing grand visions and innovative concepts that dwell in a realm of creativity. These "castles" represent the potential solutions and ideas that spark inspiration and enthusiasm.

However, the challenge lies in transitioning from this ethereal domain to reality. Just as one must carefully navigate the complexities of construction to ensure that these castles can stand firm on land, engineers and creators must rigorously analyse and test their abstract ideas. This involves rigorous reasoning, empirical evidence, and practical experimentation to validate their concepts.

The process often includes establishing correlations, conducting Finite Element Analysis (FEA), and, most importantly, creating prototypes that allow for hands-on testing. Abstract thoughts are transformed into tangible results, ensuring that what was once a dream becomes functional and reliable.

Ultimately, this transition embodies the artistry of engineering and innovation, where creativity meets practicality, and the castles in the air are beautifully grounded in the reality of proven solutions.

The Approach to Engineering Problem-Solving

Solving an engineering problem involves reasoning and constructing to make your abstract reliable. Proof is generated using established correlations, FEA, and most importantly, testing the mock-up/prototype.

This process begins by analysing the problem to develop theoretical models and potential solutions. Engineers rely on established correlations from prior research and empirical data to substantiate these ideas, which provide a solid foundation for their work.

The key techniques used in this process include:

1. Established Correlations: Utilising known relationships and data from previous studies helps to

inform the design process and predict outcomes more accurately.

2. Finite Element Analysis (FEA): This computational technique enables engineers to simulate the behaviour of materials and structures under various conditions. FEA provides insights into stress distribution, deformation, and potential failure points, allowing for optimisations before physical prototypes are developed.

3. Prototyping and Mock-up Testing: The most critical phase in solving engineering problems is the hands-on testing of prototypes or mock-ups. This practical approach allows engineers to evaluate the performance of their designs in real-world scenarios. It is through this testing that concepts are validated, shortcomings are identified, and valuable feedback is obtained.

4. Iterative Design Process: After testing, engineers often revisit their designs based on the results. This iterative process may involve refining the abstract ideas, adjusting the model, or making enhancements to ensure the solution is effective and reliable.

In conclusion, solving an engineering problem is a multifaceted endeavour that integrates reasoning, established scientific principles, simulations through FEA and rigorous testing of prototypes. Each step plays a crucial role in generating proof of concept, ultimately leading to successful and practical engineering solutions.

Building Castles in The Air: Embracing Abstract Thinking in Innovation

In the domain of innovation and problem-solving, the concept of 'building castles in the air' takes on a new significance as a metaphor for out-of-the-box thinking and abstract generation. This unconventional approach to creativity encourages individuals to explore imaginative and visionary ideas that may seem lofty or impractical at first glance but have the potential to spark groundbreaking innovations and transformative solutions.

At its core, building castles in the air represents a departure from conventional thinking and a willingness to venture into the realm of the unknown and the unconventional. By embracing abstract thinking and allowing the mind to wander freely, individuals can unlock new perspectives, challenge existing paradigms, and envision possibilities that transcend traditional boundaries.

In the context of engineering and technology, the practice of building castles in the air can inspire engineers and innovators to push the boundaries of what is possible, envisioning futuristic solutions and disruptive technologies that have the potential to reshape industries and society at large. By daring to dream big and think boldly, engineers can break free from conventional constraints, spark unconventional ideas, and drive meaningful advancements in their fields.

Moreover, the process of building castles in the air fosters a culture of experimentation, risk-taking and resilience, encouraging individuals to embrace failure as a stepping stone to success. By exploring abstract concepts and pushing the limits of creativity, engineers can cultivate a mindset of continuous learning, growth and innovation that propels them towards new horizons of discovery and achievement.

In conclusion, building castles in the air symbolises the power of abstract thinking and out-of-the-box creativity in driving innovation and progress. By daring to dream, explore, and envision possibilities beyond the confines of reality, individuals can unleash their full creative potential, inspire transformative change, and build a future limited only by the bounds of their imagination.

Perfectionists Are the Ones Most Affected By AI

Individuals with a perfectionist nature are often significantly impacted by the advancements in AI technology. They typically set exceptionally high standards for themselves and their work, leading to a constant pursuit of flawlessness. This trait can amplify the benefits and challenges posed by AI.

On the one hand, AI can be seen as a tool that helps perfectionists achieve their goals by enhancing efficiency and accuracy. For instance, AI can automate repetitive tasks, analyse vast amounts of data, and even assist in creative processes, allowing perfectionists to focus their energy on higher-level decision-making and refinement. In this sense, AI can be an ally, enabling them to meet their high standards more efficiently.

However, the reliance on AI can also exacerbate perfectionist tendencies. The availability of tools that promise precision and perfection might lead individuals to become overly critical of their work, fearing that it will never be as flawless as what AI can produce. This fear can lead to increased anxiety and self-doubt, as perfectionists may struggle to accept that human work will always have a different quality and perspective than that generated by AI.

Additionally, the comparison to AI-generated outputs can diminish the perceived value of human creativity and intuition. Perfectionists may find themselves caught in a cycle of constantly refining their work in pursuit of unattainable standards, leading to burnout and dissatisfaction. This pressure can stifle creativity and innovation, as perfectionists may become hesitant to take risks or experiment with new ideas out of fear of making mistakes.

To navigate these challenges, perfectionists need to cultivate a mindset that recognises the unique strengths of human contributions while embracing the efficiencies offered by AI. By focusing on progress rather than perfection, individuals can leverage AI as a supportive tool rather than a source of pressure. Building self-compassion and celebrating small achievements can help mitigate the difficulties associated with perfectionism in an age dominated by technology.

In summary, while AI offers numerous advantages, it also presents challenges for perfectionists. Striking a balance between leveraging AI's capabilities and maintaining a healthy perspective on personal achievements can empower perfectionists to thrive in a rapidly evolving landscape.

Conflict As the Father of Creativity

Conflict is often regarded as the father of creativity, catalysing troubleshooting, and solution-finding. When differing perspectives, ideas or challenges arise, they create a dynamic environment that encourages individuals to think critically and innovate.

In times of conflict, whether in collaboration, problem-solving or personal endeavours, the necessity to address issues can lead to groundbreaking ideas. This tension prompts individuals to push boundaries, explore new avenues and challenge the status quo. It is through this process of grappling with difficulties that creative solutions often emerge.

Moreover, conflict fosters dialogue and collaboration, allowing diverse viewpoints to converge. As teams or individuals engage in constructive discussion, they can synthesise ideas, leading to unique insights that might not have surfaced in a harmonious setting.

Ultimately, embracing conflict not only enhances creativity but also cultivates resilience and adaptability. The journey of navigating through challenges can transform obstacles into stepping stones, paving the way for innovation and progress.

Seeing Beyond: The Art of Perception and The Pursuit of Objectivity

In a world filled with distractions and preconceptions, the ability to see beyond the obvious is a rare and extraordinary skill. This capability distinguishes those who can navigate life's complexities with greater wisdom and creativity from those who are confined by their biases. While many people view the world only through the lens of what they want to see, there lies a visionary few who can perceive what others cannot. This ability stems from a conscious effort to transcend personal biases and engage more thoughtfully and imaginatively with the world.

Seeing beyond immediate appearances requires cultivating openness, critical thinking, and empathy. These qualities enable individuals to gain unique insights and a deeper understanding of their surroundings. But how can we avoid bias and approach situations without preconceived notions? This question underscores the importance of developing an unbiased perspective.

Bias, in its many forms, influences our decision-making and perception. Whether it is confirmation bias, where we favour information that confirms our existing beliefs, or the anchoring effect, where we rely too heavily on the first piece of information we receive, biases pervade our thought processes. To minimise their impact, it is crucial to be aware of these inherent tendencies. Self-awareness is the first step towards broadening our perspectives and questioning our assumptions.

Critical thinking is essential for making sound judgments. It involves objectively analysing information, evaluating evidence, and drawing reasoned conclusions. This process necessitates questioning assumptions and considering multiple viewpoints. People with extensive experience or expertise in certain areas are often better at making informed judgments. Their encounters with various scenarios provide them with a wealth of knowledge and insights, which they can apply to new situations.

Reflecting on this, it becomes evident that those who can see beyond what others cannot possess an invaluable ability to navigate the complexities of life. They leverage their imagination and critical thinking skills to look past biases and make well-founded judgments. This capability is not just about intelligence; it is about the willingness to challenge one's own beliefs and remain open to new ideas.

Imagination plays a crucial role in transcending the present reality and envisioning potential futures. This ability is particularly useful in predicting trends, anticipating challenges, and discovering innovative solutions. Creative thinking allows individuals to connect disparate pieces of information, leading to novel insights and predictions that others might overlook. This skill is invaluable in fields ranging from scientific research to business strategy.

Imaginative thinkers often excel at recognising patterns that others miss, which is crucial for accurate forecasting. By envisioning various scenarios and outcomes, they prepare for different possibilities and improve their decision-making accuracy. This foresight is particularly beneficial for leaders and analysts who need to anticipate market shifts and changes in consumer behaviour.

Leaders who can see beyond biases make more strategic decisions, positioning their organisations for long-term success. They anticipate market dynamics and adapt to changing conditions more effectively. Researchers who question assumptions and employ imaginative thinking are more likely to achieve groundbreaking discoveries and advancements.

On a personal level, individuals who recognise their biases and develop sound judgment build healthier, more empathetic relationships. They make better life choices, considering the broader impact of their decisions. Combining sound judgment with imaginative thinking enables individuals to make more accurate predictions and informed decisions, enriching both their personal and professional lives.

Ultimately, those who can see what others cannot possess a rare and invaluable ability, shaping a future that holds endless possibilities.

Approaching A Situation Without Bias

Approaching a situation without preconceptions about what transpired is a hallmark of being unbiased. This means setting aside personal feelings, previous experiences and societal influences that could colour one's judgment or perception of events. An unbiased individual seeks to understand the facts as they are, not as they wish them to be or as others have portrayed them. This approach requires a conscious effort to remain open-minded, allowing for a fair and objective assessment of the situation at hand.

Being unbiased is particularly crucial in scenarios where decisions or judgments need to be made. Whether in a professional setting, such as legal proceedings or academic research, or in everyday life, like resolving conflicts or consuming news, an unbiased stance helps to ensure that conclusions are based on evidence and reason rather than prejudice or emotion.

Moreover, maintaining an unbiased perspective promotes critical thinking and empathy. It encourages individuals to consider multiple viewpoints and to recognise the complexity of the situation. Rather than jumping to conclusions or siding with one perspective over another prematurely, an unbiased person acknowledges the nuances and seeks to understand the motivations and circumstances behind different positions.

However, achieving true unbiasedness is challenging. Humans are naturally inclined to have biases, many of which are unconscious and shaped by our backgrounds, cultures, and personal experiences. Being aware of these biases and actively working to mitigate their influence is a continuous process, requiring self-reflection and a commitment to fairness and open-mindedness.

Ultimately, striving to be unbiased enhances the quality of our interactions and decisions. It fosters a more inclusive, just and understanding environment, where diverse perspectives are considered, and decisions are made based on a comprehensive understanding of the facts.

Addressing Opposition to Controversies, Challenging Established Norms

In any organisation or community, challenging established norms can evoke a spectrum of reactions, ranging from enthusiastic support to strong opposition. This dynamic is particularly evident in discussions surrounding controversial topics that seek to question or redefine long-held beliefs and practices. Addressing this opposition requires a thoughtful approach that promotes open dialogue, fosters understanding and encourages constructive engagement.

1. Recognising the importance of diverse perspectives

Acknowledging that opposition often stems from deeply rooted values or experiences is crucial. When addressing controversies, it is important to create an environment where differing viewpoints are recognised as valuable contributions to the discussion. Encouraging team members or stakeholders to share their perspectives can lead to a richer understanding of the issue at hand, as well as highlight potential blind spots.

2. Facilitating open dialogue

Creating a safe space for discussion is essential when dealing with controversies. Implementing structured formats for dialogue - such as roundtable discussions, workshops, or moderated debates - can help ensure that all voices are heard. By establishing ground rules that emphasise respect and active listening, participants are more likely to engage in constructive conversations rather than confrontational arguments.

3. Employing Emotional Intelligence

Using Emotional Intelligence to navigate these discussions is key. Leaders and facilitators should be attuned to the emotions and reactions of participants, demonstrating empathy, and validating their feelings. By addressing concerns with sensitivity and understanding, it is possible to reduce defensiveness and promote a more collaborative atmosphere. This involves asking open-ended questions, reflecting on participants' responses, and acknowledging the emotional weight of certain topics.

4. Providing clear and evidence-based information

Often, opposition arises from misinformation or a lack of understanding about the issues being discussed. Providing clear, well-researched and balanced information can help demystify complex topics and reduce fear or resistance. Incorporating expert opinions, case studies and data can assist in grounding the conversation in facts rather than perceptions, leading to more informed decision-making.

5. Encouraging critical thinking

Instead of advocating for blind acceptance of new ideas, the aim should be to promote critical thinking. Encouraging participants to ask questions, challenge assumptions and weigh the pros and cons of established norms against proposed changes fosters a culture of inquiry. By empowering individuals to think critically about the implications of both maintaining the status quo and embracing change, teams can arrive at more nuanced, well-reasoned conclusions.

6. Finding common ground

In discussions where emotions run high, it is essential to identify shared values and goals. By highlighting common interests, participants may find it easier to bridge divisions and work collaboratively towards solutions. This can involve reframing the conversation to focus on collective objectives, which often helps diffuse tension and fosters a sense of unity.

7. Creating actionable pathways

Lastly, addressing opposition effectively requires creating actionable pathways for moving forward. This could involve developing a consensus on certain points, proposing pilot programs for new ideas or establishing metrics to evaluate the impact of changes. By providing clear next steps, participants can feel empowered to take constructive action rather than remaining mired in conflict.

In conclusion, addressing opposition to controversies that challenge established norms is a complex but necessary endeavour. By fostering an environment of open dialogue, utilising Emotional Intelligence, providing clear information and encouraging critical thinking, teams can navigate these discussions productively. Ultimately, embracing diverse perspectives can lead to innovation, growth, and a more engaged community.

Emotional Quotient (EQ) Over Intelligence Quotient (IQ)

Prioritising EQ while leveraging AI for tasks that heavily rely on IQ could create a more balanced and practical approach in both personal and professional environments.

In the workplace, human roles are focused on EQ. For example, leaders with high EQ can inspire, motivate, and understand their team members, fostering a positive and productive work environment. In customer service, empathetic interactions with customers can enhance satisfaction and loyalty. Additionally, in collaboration and teamwork, building strong relationships and managing conflicts effectively requires high EQ.

On the other hand, AI roles are focused on IQ. For example, in data analysis, AI can process vast amounts of data quickly and accurately, identifying patterns and insights that might be missed by humans. Also, automating routine tasks frees human resources to focus on more complex and emotionally driven activities. In problem-solving, a combination of the human touch and AI can provide efficient solutions and decision-making support for well-defined and logical problems.

Jobless

Him: Hey, what are you up to these days?

Me: I am jobless, automation has taken over.

Him: Let us go watch a flick.

Me: Are you kidding? I cannot sit still unless there is an argument.

Him: You are nuts! I am normal, what good can you do be so restless?

Me: Restlessness in old age can be a sign of retained reflexes. Am I good for nothing?

Him: No! I did not say that, you are the most creative person I know with a list of patents and a series of PVP presentations at ASME. You can do a lot when you are sober.

Me: I did all that because I did what I was not supposed to do.

Him: That does not make sense.

Me: Unless you're pushed to the wall, your mind doesn't work.

Him: Why?

Me: What will you come out of unless you put yourself in trouble?

Him: I see what you're saying, but isn't there a way to channel that restlessness into something more constructive?

Me: Absolutely, I believe that restlessness can be a driving force for creativity and innovation. It's about finding the right balance between pushing boundaries and staying grounded.

Him: So, you think conflict is necessary for creativity to thrive?

Me: Yes, I do. Conflict challenges our perspectives, forces us to think differently, and ultimately leads to new ideas and solutions. It's like a spark that ignites the creative process.

Him: That's an interesting way to look at it. Maybe I should embrace a bit more restlessness and conflict in my own life.

Me: It's worth exploring. Sometimes stepping out of our comfort zones and embracing challenges can lead to unexpected growth and success.

Him: Thanks for the insight. Let's continue this conversation over that flick we were talking about earlier.

Me: Sounds like a plan! I'm always up for a good debate, even in a movie theatre. Which is the movie?

Him: Anban - The Soulmates.

Earning More Is Worth It

Seeing Tema India strive to increase revenue fills us with motivation, knowing that the fruits of our labour will be channelled towards empowering the youth through our CSR initiatives. The happiness that comes from witnessing young minds being nurtured and empowered is a powerful driving force, inspiring us to work harder and make a positive impact in the lives of others.

Our motivation is intricately tied to the vision of Tema India not just surviving, but thriving and reaching new heights of technology and financial success. This success not only opens new opportunities but also allows us to witness the profound impact it has on the youth involved in our CSR initiatives.

Sharing our surplus with others in need is like a weight lifted off our shoulders, bringing a sense of fulfilment and purpose that goes beyond material wealth. It is in these acts of generosity and kindness that we find true happiness and make a positive impact on the world around us.

The Essence Of Management

Resolve problems, not create them

Learn to resolve problems, not create them. The blame game is counterproductive and only serves to escalate tensions and hinder progress. Instead, focus on the issues at hand, not the person. By addressing the root cause of the problem and working collaboratively, we can find effective solutions that benefit everyone involved. Constructive criticism, open communication, and a commitment to understanding different perspectives are key to fostering a positive and productive environment.

Do not run away from a situation

Having taken up a responsibility, do not run away from a situation. See it through before you consider abandoning the charge. Embracing responsibility means facing challenges head-on and demonstrating resilience, even when the going gets tough. It is easy to walk away when things become difficult, but true growth and leadership come from navigating through adversity and finding solutions. By committing to see things through, you not only fulfil your obligations but also build trust and respect among your peers. Remember, perseverance in the face of challenges often leads to personal and professional growth, and it sets a positive example for others to follow.

Influencing a colleague for ulterior motives is a serious offense

When top management forms a panel of experienced individuals to complete a task, influencing a participant for ulterior motives is a serious offense. Such actions undermine the integrity of the process and can lead to biased decisions that are not in the best interest of the organisation. Ethical conduct and transparency are paramount in ensuring that the panel can operate effectively and make decisions based on merit and objective analysis. Any attempt to sway a participant for personal gain not only compromises the task at hand but also erodes trust within the organisation. All members need to uphold the highest standards of professionalism and ethics to maintain the credibility and effectiveness of the panel's work. Violations of this trust should be addressed promptly and appropriately to preserve the organisation's integrity and the confidence of all stakeholders.

Changing horses midstream can bring a project to a grinding halt

Changing horses midstream can bring a project to a grinding halt. The responsibility lies in taking well-calculated risks and thoroughly investigating the consequences, which must be addressed firmly. When a project is underway, sudden changes in strategy, personnel or resources can disrupt progress and lead to confusion, delays, and potential failure. It is crucial to weigh the potential benefits against the risks and to have contingency plans in place. Decision-makers must conduct a thorough analysis of the possible outcomes and ensure that any changes are necessary and justified. Clear communication and detailed planning are essential to mitigate the impact of such changes and to keep the project on track.

Unconventional solutions often emerge when logic becomes redundant

Those who approach situations with impartiality and objectivity typically do not harbour concerns or anxieties, as their judgments are based on fair and unbiased assessments. On the other hand, individuals who exhibit bias in their decision-making processes may cause unease or apprehension due to the potential for unfairness or partiality in their actions.

When traditional methods and logical reasoning fail to provide a satisfactory solution, thinking outside the box becomes essential. It is in these moments of uncertainty and unconventional thinking that innovative and creative solutions can be discovered. By breaking free from the constraints of traditional approaches, new possibilities and perspectives can be explored, leading to fresh insights and breakthrough solutions.

Resource planning

Resource planning is the strategic process of coordinating the delivery schedules and allocation of resources across various divisions within an umbrella company. This involves ensuring that each division receives the necessary resources (such as labour, space, and machinery) in a timely and efficient manner to meet their operational and production goals. Effective resource planning aims to optimise the use of available resources, minimise costs, reduce delays and enhance overall productivity across the entire organisation.

Despite planning, we have no control over external circumstances

While careful planning serves as a foundational element in achieving goals, it is important to recognise the inherent limitations of our control over circumstances. Life is often shaped by unforeseen events, shifting dynamics and factors beyond our immediate influence. Despite our best efforts and intentions, the outcomes of our plans can be profoundly affected by external realities that are often unpredictable.

Acknowledging the uncertainty inherent in life encourages resilience and creativity. By adopting a mindset that welcomes change and embraces the unknown, we empower ourselves to respond more effectively to challenges. This adaptability not only enhances problem-solving abilities but also promotes personal growth and the ability to navigate life's complexities with grace.

Leadership involves developing a second-in-command

True leadership involves not just guiding a team but also developing the second-in-command to a level where the leader becomes dispensable. This process is vital for the sustainability and growth of any organisation. By mentoring and empowering a second-in-command, leaders create a sense of continuity and stability, ensuring that the team can thrive even in their absence.

Moreover, having a strong second-in-command enables leaders to delegate responsibilities effectively, allowing them to focus on strategic vision and long-term goals. It encourages a culture of collaboration, where innovation and creative problem-solving are prioritised. Ultimately, the goal of a leader should be to create an ecosystem where leadership skills are shared and nurtured, leading to a more resilient and adaptive organisation. This approach not only benefits the current team but also sets the stage for future leaders to emerge, ensuring the continued success and longevity of the organisation.

Going public

An organisation goes public through an Initial Public Offering (IPO) when it decides to sell shares of stock to the public for the first time. This process allows the company to raise capital to fund business operations, expansion, or other strategic initiatives. Going public also provides an opportunity for early investors and founders to realise their investment by selling their shares, and it can increase the company's visibility and prestige in the market.

Before going public, it is crucial to understand the purpose and commitment to it. Go public if you see your shareholders as a community you belong to and wish to stand with for generations to come. Otherwise, it is akin to running for shelter and not having the confidence to face the heat by ploughing back your earnings.

Our company Tema India has an outstanding track record of paying bonuses and ex gratia to staff and workmen on time for the past 54 years. This reflects not just a commitment to financial punctuality but a deeper testament to the value we place on all members of our team. To go public, our CMD is prepared to mortgage all personal property in place of the first charge of the company.

As we consider taking this pivotal step toward an IPO, it is important to know that this move is about more than just capital. This significant step exemplifies an unwavering belief in our mission and a resolute commitment to our community of shareholders.

The Impact of The Environment on Workers

Understanding and addressing the impact of the environment on the lives of workers is crucial for creating a sustainable and healthy workplace. By acknowledging and mitigating the effects of environmental factors on employees, companies can greatly improve the well-being and productivity of both, blue-collar and white-collar workers.

For blue-collar workers, implementing environmentally-friendly practices can lead to a safer and more comfortable work environment. This can result in reduced health risks, fewer accidents, and increased job satisfaction among workers. By prioritising the well-being of blue-collar employees, companies can boost morale and productivity on the factory floor or in the field.

Similarly, for white-collar workers, promoting a sustainable work culture can enhance job satisfaction and overall performance. By incorporating green initiatives and practices, such as energy-efficient technologies and waste-reduction programs, companies can empower employees to make a positive impact on the environment. This sense of purpose and responsibility can lead to increased motivation, creativity, and innovation in their roles.

Furthermore, planting trees serves as a tangible and impactful way to combat climate change and promote environmental sustainability. By investing in tree-planting initiatives, companies can not only offset their carbon footprint but also contribute to cleaner air, improved biodiversity, and a healthier planet for future generations. Embracing tree planting as a forward-thinking strategy demonstrates a commitment to environmental stewardship and sets a positive example for employees and the community.

Focusing on environmental impact in the workplace can also catalyse the generation of creative ideas and innovative solutions. When employees are encouraged to think about sustainability and environmental responsibility, it can spark creativity and inspire them to come up with new ways to reduce waste, conserve resources and minimize the company's carbon footprint.

Creating a culture that values sustainability can lead to brainstorming sessions, collaborative projects and cross-functional initiatives aimed at finding creative solutions to environmental challenges. Employees from different departments and backgrounds can come together to share ideas, experiment with new technologies and implement sustainable practices that benefit the company and the environment.

By fostering a culture of creativity and innovation around environmental impact, companies can tap into the diverse perspectives and talents of their workforce to drive positive change and make a meaningful impact on the planet. Improving environmental practices in the workplace can have a positive impact on productivity. By creating a healthier and more sustainable work environment, employees are likely to experience fewer health issues related to poor air quality or exposure to harmful substances. This can lead to reduced absenteeism, increased morale, and higher job satisfaction among workers.

The environmental impact in the lives of workmen can be significant, as their work activities may contribute to pollution, resource depletion, and other environmental issues. Companies need to consider the environmental impact of their operations on workmen and take steps to minimise negative effects through sustainable practices, proper waste management and promoting eco-friendly initiatives. By prioritising environmental responsibility, companies can create a healthier and more sustainable work environment for their employees.

Forestry: Our Corporate Social Responsibility

Asia is home to the world's 100 most polluted cities, with a staggering 83 of them in India. This alarming statistic serves as a wake-up call for organisations to act and make a difference through their CSR initiatives.

At Tema India, we are committed to addressing this environmental crisis. We believe that forestry holds the key to sustainable change and by focussing on it, we aim to combat pollution, promote environmental conservation, and support wildlife.

By planting trees, conserving forests, supporting reforestation efforts, and advocating for sustainable forestry practices, organisations can make a tangible impact on the environment and society. These initiatives not only help in reducing pollution but also create a positive ripple effect on the community.

We are proud to say that at our three manufacturing setups located in Talasari (Maharashtra), Kherdi (Dadra & Nagar Haveli) and Panoli (Gujarat), we have embarked on a journey of forestation as part of our commitment to CSR and environmental sustainability.

Through our forestation initiatives, we are not only addressing the challenges of pollution and environmental degradation but also creating a positive impact on our communities and the ecosystem. We believe that by taking proactive steps towards sustainable practices, we can pave the way for a greener, healthier future for all.

We invite you to visit our manufacturing setups, witness our forestation efforts first-hand, and explore opportunities for collaboration and knowledge sharing. Together, we can drive positive change and make a meaningful difference in our environment.

Join us in our mission to lead the way in sustainable practices and create a brighter future for the generations to come.

The Heart of CSR

In the heart of CSR, forestry stands tall,
A commitment to nature, heeding the call.
Planting trees with care, for one and all,
Sustaining the earth, where creatures crawl.

Rooted in purpose, a forest's embrace,
Conserving the land, a sacred space.
Reforestation blooms, a hopeful trace,
Of a greener world, for every race.

Through the canopy's whisper, a promise is made,
To nurture the earth, in the forest's shade.
In the realm of CSR, where actions cascade,
Forestry's legacy, in every glade.

Epilogue

The heart inspires the mind to strive for achievement, blending passion with purpose to create extraordinary results.

The Story of Tapan Ghosh: The Alter Ego of Haresh Sippy, the visionary founder of Tema India, stands at the intersection of engineering excellence and creative exploration. His professional world is marked by precision, innovation, and problem-solving. Yet, behind this structured exterior exists his alter ego, Tapan Ghosh—a maverick storyteller and filmmaker who thrives on breaking conventions and exploring the depths of human emotion. Tapan Ghosh embodies the chaos, spontaneity, and daring that Haresh Sippy's corporate persona often tempers. While Haresh focuses on creating cutting-edge engineering solutions, Tapan immerses himself in crafting narratives that confront societal norms, explore human vulnerability, and challenge traditional thinking. Their relationship is not without tension. Tapan's creative ventures often highlight conflicts—between tradition and modernity, logic and emotion, and innovation and convention. These conflicts, however, are not destructive; they are catalytic. Haresh Sippy leverages the lessons from Tapan's imaginative explorations to foster innovation in engineering. By analyzing the conflicts Tapan creates in his art, Haresh gains new perspectives on problem-solving and teamwork.

For instance:

• Challenging Norms: Tapan's stories often question established norms, inspiring Haresh to rethink traditional engineering practices and embrace cutting-edge technologies, such as 3D printing and automation.

• Creative Problem-Solving: The dramatic tension in Tapan's narratives translates into Haresh's ability to approach engineering challenges with creativity and adaptability, ensuring solutions that are both efficient and effective.

• Empathy and Collaboration: Tapan's exploration of human emotions deepens Haresh's understanding of teamwork, fostering a culture where diverse perspectives drive innovation within Tema India. In turn, Haresh's discipline and analytical thinking provide Tapan with a structured foundation for his artistic endeavors.

The precision of engineering becomes the backbone of Tapan's experimental cinema, ensuring that his stories, though bold and unconventional, resonate with universal truths and practical wisdom. Together, Haresh Sippy and Tapan Ghosh demonstrate that conflict, when analyzed and embraced, can lead to growth and discovery. This dynamic interplay has not only enriched their personal and professional lives but has also redefined how engineering and art can influence each other. Through their duality, they build not just machines and movies but a legacy of innovation and creativity. Haresh enhances Tema India with insights drawn from Tapan's creative chaos, while Tapan's stories are imbued with the wisdom gained from Haresh's engineering triumphs. In their journey, they prove that the key to innovation lies in the heart of conflict, where passion and logic merge to create extraordinary results.

www.ingramcontent.com/pod-product-compliance
Lightning Source LLC
LaVergne TN
LVHW091538070526
838199LV00002B/112